Dan,

This is a wonderful testimony of Gods protection and His very Presence with All our Troops in this on-going war of our generation. After you finish it. "Pass it on" and share it with others -

These simple pieces of cloth (Bandanas) with God's words has saved lives and given Eternal Life to many of our soldiers!

Love,

your sister

Lovin' Our Troops

A Story of Service on Two Fronts

MARY BASS GRAY

CROSSBOOKS
PUBLISHING

CrossBooks™
A Division of LifeWay
1663 Liberty Drive
Bloomington, IN 47403
www.crossbooks.com
Phone: 1-866-879-0502

Operation Bandanas
PO Box 87356
Fayetteville, NC 28304
bandanas91@yahoo.com
www.operationbandanas.org

First published by CrossBooks 04/02/2012

ISBN: 978-1-4627-1470-4 (sc)
ISBN: 978-1-4627-1471-1 (hc)
ISBN: 978-1-4627-1472-8 (e)

Library of Congress Control Number: 2012904208

Printed in the United States of America

This book is printed on acid-free paper.

Dedicated to the extraordinary men and women of the United States Armed Forces and to the families and friends who support them.

CONTENTS

INTRODUCTION

It all began as a journey of faith in Fayetteville, North Carolina, in November, 2006. But actually, looking back on the journey and the mileposts set up along the way, my life was moving me toward this juncture for quite some time. Mileposts show distance and how far you have come. I've come a long way since the day I said "I do" to someone about to begin a career in the U.S. Army.

I've had a long and personal relationship with our military: from being a military wife for twenty years, accompanying my retired Vietnam veteran on sixteen moves all across America and an ocean and experiencing the separation that war brings; to birthing three sons who became a part of the military family. Two sons have actively served in our military and have experienced multiple deployments to Iraq and Afghanistan since 9/11. I understand the needs of these young men and women, for their physical, emotional, and spiritual well-being.

Lovin' Our Troops is all about our military and a special calling I received for ministering to them. I have had special callings and significant events throughout my life journey. And there are those mileposts all along the way, those markers or milestones that were turning points in my life that I encountered. *Lovin' Our Troops* is the story of one of those encounters. It is a personal story about being given an opportunity to serve, from the home front, those serving on the battle front.

I was called to provide a small, simple item, that has potentially powerful possibilities to change and impact lives. God can take the smallest thing and use it for something big, for some Higher purpose that is beyond our imagining. And He can call an ordinary person like me to join Him to propel his Higher purpose. From personal experiences, emails, and journals, you will catch a glimpse into the extraordinary service and sacrifices being made by our military of all branches and how much this simple item, a Psalm 91 bandana, came to mean to them.

Journey with me now!

CHAPTER 1

The Journey Begins

I had the privilege of being an army wife for twenty years. And what an amazing journey it was! My husband, Eastland, was commissioned into the U.S. Army upon graduation from college in 1968. I'd just finished my freshman year in college although we had been dating since high school. He said he wasn't about to leave me behind for some other guy to snatch away; so he proposed. We were married the summer after he graduated.

As a young bride, I was filled with excitement at the idea of moving to a new place and beginning our married life and our army adventure together. We moved into a very small apartment in Columbus, Georgia, for Eastland to attend the Infantry Officers Basic Course (IOBC) at Ft. Benning. While our start was humble and not very glamorous, we have fond memories of those early days. We'd both lived all of our lives in the same hometown with all of our family around us. Now we were striking out on our own! I was nineteen years old, young, naive, and sheltered. I still had a lot of growing up to do. I didn't know anything about being an officer's wife in the U.S. Army. I had a lot to learn, but I was in love with my Second Lieutenant and happy to be alongside him. (While in the army, Eastland went by his first name, Woods, as is the custom when you are in the military. If anyone reading this book knew us back then while on active duty, then he is Woods to you!)

In 1969, we moved to Baltimore, Maryland, for Eastland to attend training at Ft. Holabird. Upon completion of training, we were assigned to Ft. Richardson, Alaska. After a year in Alaska, Eastland received his orders for Vietnam. We moved to Ft. Bliss, Texas, for him to attend language school, and when he departed for Vietnam in 1970, I moved back home with my parents. That was five moves in 2 ½ years!

Upon Eastland's return from Vietnam, and after the advanced course at Ft. Huachuca, Arizona, we received orders for an assignment to England. I was excited, yet somewhat apprehensive as I prepared to embark on this big move. I was pregnant with our first child; and I would be living in a foreign country, far away from family and all I was accustomed to in America. But one night God brought to my mind a passage of Scripture that reminded me that no matter where I went, He would be with me. I didn't need to be afraid or worried. "Where can I go from your Spirit? Where can I flee from your presence? If I go up to the heavens, you are there; if I make my bed in the depths, you are there. If I rise on the wings of the dawn, if I settle on the far side of the sea, even there your hand will guide me, your right hand will hold me fast" (Psalm 139:7-10, NIV). Wherever we went -- even across an ocean -- I had the peace of knowing that God was there preparing the way for us. That little expression, "Bloom where you're planted," became a way of life for me!

The birth of three sons, Robert, Michael, and Andrew --two of whom would also join the U.S. Army --were significant milestones during that time. Our oldest son is a career soldier and our youngest honorably served in the army for 5 ½ years and is now a veteran of two long tours in Afghanistan. Our middle son served overseas with the Peace Corps after graduating from college before embarking on his full time career. Service to God, country, family, and community has always been a part of our family values.

God is always preparing us for the next milepost on the journey. It is evident to me as I look back that the story I am about to share was being put into place even way back then in 1968.

CHAPTER 2

Just a Thought—I Thought

"War is a terrible tragedy, and we must do all we can to strive for peace in our world. But sometimes the only way to achieve peace is to fight those who would take it from us."
- Billy Graham, *My Answer*, Memorial Day, 2011

My husband has been to war. As mentioned in the previous chapter, he is a Vietnam veteran. Two of our three sons have been to war, serving in Operation Enduring Freedom in Afghanistan and Operation Iraqi Freedom in Iraq. They've joined with the one percent of our nation who wears the uniform of our armed forces and are well trained and ready to do whatever it takes to ensure freedom and safety both at home and around the world.

I think they would tell you that their job is more about saving lives than taking lives. It is more about achieving peace than making war, but if necessary, taking the fight to those who would take peace from us. Our soldiers, sailors, airmen and marines bear arms both to defend our nation and to bring freedom to the oppressed. They are not eager nor are they looking for opportunities to wage war on others. They are defenders who respond to threats. If need be, they will fight to achieve peace.

In addition to having two warrior sons, I have a son who works in embassies around the world as a foreign service officer with the Department of State, striving for peace through diplomacy. All three of my sons continue to serve their nation in some capacity, and I am very proud of them. As the wife of a retired soldier and the mother of two warriors and a diplomat, I pray for peace so that wars will cease. But as a Christian, I don't believe that

3

will ever happen until Christ Himself returns to earth. And so, we send sons, daughters, husbands, fathers, brothers, sisters, loved ones, and friends off to do battle for us. Most are young; all are brave.

In 2006, our oldest son, Rob, deployed to Iraq. It was a third deployment for him in that part of the world. As a mother, I wanted to encourage my son in any way possible--with gifts and goody boxes; through prayers, e-mails, and letters; and through words of encouragement. As a Christian mother, I particularly wanted to encourage him spiritually. War hits hard physically, emotionally, and spiritually. I couldn't be there to physically protect my son (as any momma would if she could); I couldn't help him cope emotionally with the horrors he may experience. But I could bear him up on the wings of prayer asking for God's physical, emotional, and spiritual protection over him.

While surfing the Internet, I found the website, www.dreamci.com (now, www.thepsalm91bandana.com), which sold military camouflage bandanas imprinted with Psalm 91. Psalm 91 is a psalm of protection and has been called the soldiers' psalm. It reminds all who read it that God is their refuge and their fortress, their shield, their secret place, their cover, their deliverance, and their salvation. It's a psalm of comfort, courage, and strength--words that I knew would encourage my son spiritually and remind him that God was always with him. I immediately ordered several to send Rob--one for him and a few extra to share with his battle buddies. Little did I know that this would be the beginning of my present marker on the journey, a special calling that would end up blessing not only my son, but many thousands of other sons and daughters serving in Iraq and Afghanistan.

I mailed Rob his package of Psalm 91 bandanas in October, 2006. Seeing so many soldiers on duty and deploying almost continuously from Ft. Bragg, I couldn't help but think how wonderful it would be for them to receive Psalm 91 bandanas too. It was just a thought --or so I thought! God had already set His plan in motion by moving us to Fayetteville in 2005, and it required our becoming part of a military community to fulfill it.

CHAPTER 3

Psalm 91

¹ He who dwells in the secret place of the Most High
Shall abide under the shadow of the Almighty.
² I will say of the LORD, "He is my refuge and my fortress;
My God, in Him I will trust."
³ Surely He shall deliver you from the snare of the fowler
And from the perilous pestilence.
⁴ He shall cover you with His feathers,
And under His wings you shall take refuge;
His truth shall be your shield and buckler.
⁵ You shall not be afraid of the terror by night,
Nor of the arrow that flies by day,
⁶ Nor of the pestilence that walks in darkness,
Nor of the destruction that lays waste at noonday.
⁷ A thousand may fall at your side,
And ten thousand at your right hand;
But it shall not come near you.
⁸ Only with your eyes shall you look,
And see the reward of the wicked.
⁹ Because you have made the LORD, who is my refuge,
Even the Most High, your dwelling place,
¹⁰ No evil shall befall you,
Nor shall any plague come near your dwelling;
¹¹ For He shall give His angels charge over you,

To keep you in all your ways.
[12] In their hands they shall bear you up,
Lest you dash your foot against a stone.
[13] You shall tread upon the lion and the cobra,
The young lion and the serpent you shall trample underfoot.
[14] "Because he has set his love upon Me, therefore I will deliver him;
I will set him on high, because he has known My name.
[15] He shall call upon Me, and I will answer him;
I will be with him in trouble;
I will deliver him and honor him.
[16] With long life I will satisfy him,
And show him My salvation.

CHAPTER 4

The Call

Three weeks after sending Rob his bandanas, I awoke to begin another day. But it wasn't going to be just another ordinary day. Something extraordinary was about to happen! When my feet hit the floor and after a good long stretch, suddenly, not audibly but very clearly, God spoke to me, "Let's get bandanas for the soldiers at Ft. Bragg." My mind went blank for a moment. Once my foggy, startled brain processed that God had just spoken to me, I responded with a question -- "Well God, how am I going to do that? There are tens of thousands of troops at Ft. Bragg." (Ft. Bragg is home of the XVIII Airborne Corps, the 82nd Airborne Division and U.S. Army Special Operations Command, in addition to other strategic and support units. There are between 40,000 - 50,000 soldiers assigned to Ft. Bragg.) Immediately and very clearly, God responded to my question --"Tell my people." It's an overwhelming, humbling experience when you know you have just been given a specific assignment from God!

Often when we hear God call us to serve or fulfill a particular mission, we come up with excuses why we shouldn't or couldn't. We may even suggest He find someone else who, in our mind, is better equipped, better educated, and more capable. But God has a track record of intentionally calling the ordinary to do His extraordinary. He has done that since the beginning of time! Without any doubt I may have briefly encountered, I said, "OK, Lord, whatever you say." Saying yes to God is the only appropriate response one can make if you call Him LORD. I had zero dollars to begin purchasing bandanas for thousands of soldiers; but what I did have was a lot of faith. I knew God would provide the resources because He was orchestrating all of this. My part now was to begin telling His people as He directed me to.

A couple of days later I shared my experience with a women's Bible study that I was facilitating. A basket was passed and $85.00, the very first seed money for tHIS new ministry, was given. I was encouraged! That Sunday, I shared with my Sunday school class, The Adventure Class (what an appropriate name for followers of Christ!). They encouraged me also and took up an offering. Those combined offerings were enough money to order several hundred bandanas for an army chaplain from our church. CH(CPT) Phillip Kramer, who was in Iraq at that time, was the recipient of those first Psalm 91 bandanas. It was a joy to mail them to him. (To my non-military friends, when you see CH, that is an abbreviation for Chaplain with rank in parenthesis.) I was thankful that my Christian brothers and sisters had provided the bandanas for him. I didn't have any idea what was next or how donations would multiply. But keep in mind, God called me to get bandanas for thousands of troops at Ft. Bragg, so He had more in store! His plan would continue to unfold.

I met with the XVIII Airborne Corps Chaplain serving at Ft. Bragg at that time, CH(COL) Pat Hash. I shared about the ministry I felt called to begin for the troops at Ft. Bragg. He was very supportive and thought that would be a wonderful gift to our soldiers. We would funnel the bandanas to the troops through the chaplains. CH Hash expressed that the bandanas would be particularly meaningful to the soldiers because they would be an item provided to them personally by people in our community and area. We agreed I would bring bandanas to him as I was able, and chaplains would then pass them out to soldiers deploying to Iraq and Afghanistan. My step of faith assured me that I would be seeing more of CH Hash.

There was a friend in The Adventure Class whose husband, CH(COL) Mike Hoyt, was deployed at that time as the Command Chaplain of all U.S. Forces in Iraq. His wife, Judy, said that Mike would enjoy having Psalm 91 bandanas to take with him as he moved throughout the theater of Iraq. The Adventure Class responded again and generously gave an offering to see that CH Hoyt receive Psalm 91 bandanas. Here is the letter he so graciously wrote and what a blessing it was to receive:

1 January 07

Dear Mary,

Thank you very much for the generous gifts from the Sunday school class of the Psalm 91 bandanas. The first big box arrived Christmas Eve. Wonderful timing as I spent most of Christmas day circulating the battle space visiting troops. I passed them out with due credit to your church and class. The helicopter crew that flew me around was really taken with them and very appreciative. The other two boxes arrived last week.

I always take time to talk with troops about spiritual things and provoke many responses and results. I give away a bandana somewhere in the course of the conversation. Everyone thoroughly enjoys getting one. I've passed them out to soldiers on guard in towers, entry control points, motor pool. I gave some out after a convoy prayer I led with a team I traveled with. I passed some out to our small 0700 Sunday morning congregation. (These are the few who come after night shift or just before going on for the day. I call them the "real dedicated ones.") I've given them to several of our General Officers staff who maintain a vibrant faith in spite of a crushing schedule... and to some others who think about God if I bring Him up. Always well received, these bandanas are faith builders and sources of personal encouragement. I'm having a great time witnessing to the Truths of God and passing these along.

These are worth every penny and much more personally to every troop that gets one. Thank you for the thoughtful and expensive effort. Rest assured these are making a spiritual and personal impact on our forces.

Your fellow laborer,
Mike Hoyt
Command Chaplain
MNF-I (Multi-National Force-Iraq)
Baghdad, Iraq

Operation Bandanas has a DVD to share our ministry with churches and organizations. Here are some words that CH Hoyt personally spoke on the DVD, thanking us for the bandanas:

> "Without exception, every time I pass one of the bandanas out, the soldiers pause from whatever they are doing, take it out of the bag, look at it, and then we have some dialog about it. The conversation stops when I pull the bandana out and tell them that this is being presented to you by the citizens of the United States of America, Christians, who specifically have you in mind and prayer and have spent their money and their time to be sure these are delivered to you just to let you know they support you and they are behind your personal spiritual life. What a powerful thing that is for a soldier! It sort of becomes a hallowed relic right there. Some of them want me to pray over it with them right then. No one just takes it as more stuff and puts it in their pocket. It's a moment of spiritual history for each person that receives one. This is an emblem of care and concern from the citizens of the United States with a religious focus, and I think it's playing a very unique role in what we are doing in Iraq. Thank you very much for your contributions. Know it is being respected and well received by our great forces."

> *(The comments from CH Hoyt are his personal assessment and do not necessarily reflect the views of the Department of Defense).*

CHAPTER 5

Supporting the Surge

Just before Christmas, 2006, the 2nd Brigade Combat Team of the 82nd Airborne Division was notified that they would be the front of the "surge" into Iraq. One of their battalion commanders, LTC Tom Rogers, attended my church and knew about the Psalm 91 bandanas we had provided to CH Kramer and CH Hoyt. He came to me and said that he wanted bandanas to give to every one of his soldiers as they deployed in a few weeks. I asked how many that would be and he told me 500. I would need to have some generous donations fast to purchase them; but without hesitation, I said he would have them.

The Adventure Class responded to this request along with the Senior Adult Villagers, other Sunday school classes and individuals at my church. I received a check for $1000 from a veteran in our church who was kind and thoughtful enough to give his donation in honor of my two soldier sons, one of whom was deployed to Afghanistan at that time. One of my friends contacted her family and told them that instead of giving her gifts for Christmas please use that money instead for a donation toward providing Psalm 91 bandanas to this group of soldiers. Her family personally provided a very large number of bandanas. All gave out of the abundance of their hearts and with love and gratitude for our servicemen and women.

I want to take this opportunity to give a big thank you to my Sunday school friends who were such encouragers to me in helping launch this mission. They caught the vision and enthusiastically joined in. The Adventure Class was excited about their new adventure! Some of us in the class who were there when we took that first offering for Psalm 91 bandanas continue to look back on that time and we shake our heads in amazement at what God has done through His people five years later.

We met LTC Rogers' request--and then some! Through a contact we had with our local newspaper, an article was printed in December, 2006, (along with an embarrassingly large picture of me holding a bandana). But it attracted some attention from the community and other churches. About five weeks after my "call," we had been able to raise enough money for close to 4000 Psalm 91 bandanas for our troops. I had been happy providing that first few hundred, but I could tell we were involved in something bigger. And God was right in the middle of it all, propelling and directing tHIS ministry. Our donations for 2007 totaled $107,379.33, enabling the ministry to provide a grand total (since November, 2006) of 41,799 Psalm 91 bandanas to our troops as gifts of love and spiritual encouragement! We would be continuing into 2008! God was at work and many had joined Him in it!

In the Spring of 2007, my accountant friend advised me, as money continued to come in from all over North Carolina, that I needed to apply for a 501(c)3 non-profit designation to be held accountable for all the monies coming in. It would also give us more credibility and allow tax-deductible donations. That was the birth of Operation Bandanas for Bragg, later aka Operation Bandanas. I never imagined I would be responsible for the daily operations of a non-profit organization as Founder and Executive Director and have a Board of Directors to answer to. This was way beyond my pay grade, education, or abilities; but my availability and obedience to God's call allowed Him to equip me to do the task. I was the engine on the train, and He was the Chief Engineer! This "little engine that could" was chuggin'. And I knew it would take an awful lot of "paying passengers" on the train with me to get Psalm 91 bandanas all the way to Iraq and Afghanistan and into the hands of thousands more of our troops requesting them.

Because we were able to continue to send thousands of bandanas to our Ft. Bragg chaplains deployed to Iraq and Afghanistan throughout 2007, chaplains from other military installations that were deployed alongside Ft. Bragg troops asked where all the bandanas were coming from. The word was, "There's this lady whose name is Mary in Fayetteville, NC..." My email address was passed around, and the flood gates of requests opened! By the end of the year, we had become a nationwide military support organization! But we were unique in that we provided *spiritual* support. It was daunting how many requests I started receiving. I had more requests than I had resources to provide them! The demand far exceeded the supply. This train was picking up speed!

*This picture is very special to me because it was the very first one
I received from soldiers downrange with the bandanas!*

CHAPTER 6

Still Chuggin'

Moving into 2012, Operation Bandanas continues sending Psalm 91 bandanas to our troops serving in harm's way. Hearts and minds continue to be touched to become involved in ministering to our military through tHIS ministry. We've become a nationwide ministry of spiritual support and encouragement to all branches of our military, be they active duty, National Guard, or Reserves. At the writing of this book, we have received donations in excess of a half million dollars; and 195,000 Psalm 91 bandanas have been placed into the hands of our great soldiers, sailors, airmen, marines and coast guardsmen.

Whoever thought of the expression, "It's a God thing." was right on, because it fits perfectly when we don't know how to explain something except that it is God at work! It has been incredible for me personally to have requests for thousands of bandanas, not knowing how in the world we will be able to meet the requests; then go to the post office box and find more donations coming from people I don't know from all across North Carolina and other parts of the country! I don't even know how they are finding out about our ministry! When I do have an opportunity to ask someone how they found out about Operation Bandanas, some will say they were just surfing the Internet and found our website. (You think God might have had something to do with that?) One of my friends and Board members, LTC Alfred Lunt, USA,Ret., created our website, www.operationbandanas.org, in 2009. The far reaching technology of the Internet has been a tremendous boost in getting the message out about our ministry. Please visit it. And join us in our mission!

Why are the Psalm 91 bandanas being requested in such large numbers? As mentioned in a previous chapter, Psalm 91 is a prayer of protection, courage, and strength. It brings encouragement and inspiration to those who are already Christ followers, reminding them of God's constant presence with them and His promises to them. For those who are not Christ followers, those who have never opened the Bible, never attended church, who may even refuse a Bible from a chaplain, but will take a bandana because of its usefulness, we have an incredible opportunity to make a Kingdom difference in someone's life. I feel sure that out of curiosity, or loneliness, or fear...at some point...they will read the words printed on the bandana. We claim Isaiah 55:11 over each one that we send: "So shall My word be that goes forth from My mouth; it shall not return to me void, but it shall accomplish what I please, and it shall prosper in the thing for which I sent it."

What a faith builder this has been for me. I have always had a strong faith, but what I have experienced on this leg of my journey clearly demonstrates that whatever God begins, He will see it to completion. Until He lets me know otherwise, I will continue providing Psalm 91 bandanas for those requesting them. And it hasn't just been chaplains requesting them. Wives, mothers, and fathers have requested them for their loved ones and his/her unit. Individual soldiers have sent requests also for their battle buddies, their platoon, or their company.

OpBan's prayer is that the bandanas will guide many to the complete revelation of God, direct them to a Bible, to a chapel service, a church, a chaplain, and/or a Christian buddy that will then help lead them into a personal relationship with Jesus. What a simple, yet potentially powerful ministry --providing inspiration to those who already know Him and drawing others to Him for the first time! This note from a soldier reinforces that potential: *"I'm deployed to Afghanistan and recently received one of your bandanas. It was nice of you guys. I'm not a very religious person, but your small gesture has motivated me to look more into it."* That's what I'm talking about!

15

Another thing I have learned from this experience: I have been reminded that it only takes one person to accomplish what God wants to do through them if that person will take a leap of faith. What about you? Never be afraid to step out in faith to tackle something bigger than you. It's an exciting journey into the unknown!

That reminds me of a great quote by William Carey: *"Expect great things from God; attempt great things for God;"* and two Bible verses: *"Whatever you do, do it heartily, as to the Lord..."*(Colossians 3:23). And, *"Let your light so shine before men, that they may see your good works and glorify your Father in heaven"* (Matthew 5:16).

My first delivery of bandanas to a chaplain about to deploy. They needed the bandanas in a hurry so we didn't even have time to fold and package them.

CHAPTER 7

Encouraging Words

North American Mission Board
4200 North Point Parkway
Alpharetta, GA 30022

September 11, 2009

To Whom It May Concern:

With thanksgiving to God I have the privilege of commending to you the ministry of Operation Bandanas under the leadership of Mary Gray. This specialized ministry of support and encouragement to military personnel provides Psalm 91 printed on a camouflaged bandana.

Bandanas are used by military personnel in a variety of ways, most often the bandana is wrapped around the head as a cushion from the helmet they wear for protection. Some will wrap the bandana around their hand and use to wipe the sweat from their brow while others will tie the bandana around the arm or leg. In all these ways the bandana represents the Word of God and declares His presence with the person and reminds the person of God's watchfulness over their life.

Operation Bandanas gets the Word of God into the hands of those who protect our great nation and our way of life. It is a gift that is readily received reminding the person that eternal life is a reality!

The Chaplaincy Team of the North American Mission Board, SBC, has been recommending Operation Bandanas for many years. We have commended Operation Bandanas to Lifeway Christian Resources for coverage in an article for Deacon Magazine coming in the spring 2010.

Mary Gray is a very active member of Village Baptist Church, Fayetteville, NC, near Ft Bragg. She serves as a Sunday school teacher and as a week day teacher in a women's Bible study group to name a few ministries in which she participates. She is certified from New Orleans Baptist Seminary in Women's Ministry.

I pray that you will join in support of Operation Bandanas.

Sincerely,

B. Keith Travis, DMin
Chaplaincy Evangelism Team Leader

I felt honored to receive this endorsement and am most appreciative for the continued support of the North American Mission Board. I would like to personally thank Dr. David B. Mullis, Chaplaincy Coordinator for NAMB, for the encouragement he has given me through the years. Lifeway Christian Resources did contact me, and Operation Bandanas was written up in *Deacon Magazine*, Summer, 2010, edition. I had a number of responses and donations from across the country from the article.

Operation Bandanas has been blessed and honored also to have become a ministry partner with Military Ministry in Newport News, Virginia, the military ministry arm of Campus Crusade for Christ. In 2010, they began including our Psalm 91 bandana in their chaplain's sample packet of free materials that they provide to chaplains. They do a wonderful job of spiritually encouraging our troops and their families through a number of ministries, resources, and partnerships, "all based on the belief that faith makes a difference in the lives of those in harm's way — those who have answered the call to serve their nations and live with the special conditions and stresses of military life, whether on the front lines or on the home front, whether before, during, or after deployments into combat." Their website is www.militaryministry.org.

CHAPTER 8

From the Front

I thought this email was especially poignant...

> "We are in an area where we are under constant contact with the enemy. One of my Soldiers sustained a bullet wound to the leg one morning and was brought into our aid station. When I walked in to visit and to pray with him, the medics had removed all of his clothes and he was completely naked except for one thing... his Psalm 91 bandana that was still tied around his forehead. I share this with you because I want you to know how important these bandanas are to my men. Your generosity means so much to them. May God bless you all richly for what you have done and continue to do for Soldiers!" CH Mark Olson

I followed up with CH Olson on this soldier:

> "He is doing well and on the road to recovery. I was out visiting one of my Companies of Soldiers this week, and as I was preparing to go on a patrol with one of the platoons, a Soldier once again thanked me for the bandanas. The last time I was there I made sure each Soldier got a couple of Bandanas. I prayed with them as they prepared to go out and then sent them on their way. The Soldier told me that on that patrol, bullets had hit the wall all around him but none hit him. Another Soldier had bullets hitting ground all around his feet, but none hit him. These Soldiers said that they will never leave the

wire again without their bandanas on. Everywhere I go, I see Soldiers wearing them. They are assured of the power of God to protect them as they continue to come back safely each time. With all the good news though is some sad news. In the last month we have lost two Soldiers and have had many others injured. My Soldiers are laying their lives on the line every time they go on a mission. Please keep them in your prayers. Thanks for all the encouragement you provide them through the bandanas you have sent and continue to send."

More emails:

"We have been in Iraq nearly a month now, and we keep a stash of the bandanas in a box of goodies that we take around to our units as they prepare for missions. The guys are always thrilled to see us, and most of the time all they want is the Chaplain's prayer and a bandana! The bandanas get snatched up faster than the candy, it seems! I can't tell you how many people see me coming and come up asking if I have any more bandanas because they know someone who needs one. It is really a beautiful part of our ministry! Thank you so much for helping us better serve our soldiers." SPC Amanda Conway, Chaplain's Asst. (Before Amanda deployed, she asked her church back home to donate to provide the bandanas to her entire battalion; and they did!)

"The desert camo 91st Psalm has been a highlight and encouragement throughout this tour. I'm very happy to have a reminder of Jesus' promise in my life. I also have enjoyed the privilege of passing out this promise to my comrades in arms. Our/my Jesus is so sweet. Thank God for people like you who love Him!" Baghdad, Iraq

"I carry my bandana with me when I go on missions, so it is always in my pocket where I can pull it out to read the

Psalm and draw on God's protection. Thank you for making a difference for the soldiers here. The more times we read Psalm 91, the more we realize that if we just give our fear and worries to God, He will protect us from harm."

"Thank you for the bandanas for my Battalion. I had my two girls, ages 8 and 6, to draw on the bandana with a marker and write stuff for me to read later. I guess you could say the bandana has more than just one purpose: It can protect from the sun, provide a canvas for the kids, and remind me of the protection that God gives to His children." CH Kevin Guthrie, Orgun-E, Afghanistan

"We are pushing the bandanas out to soldiers. It is incredible, but to think of all the things that soldiers desire in times of their need for God, they use these bandanas. They do so more than just as another TA-50 item. Many of them read the Psalm daily and find themselves meditating on it." CH(MAJ) William "Chip" Nicholas, Camp Taji, Iraq

"I received one of your bandanas today. I'm serving in Afghanistan and am constantly in hostile territory. Thank you for the bandana. I'll keep it with me always."

"I attend the Carpenter's Shop chapel at Camp Wright, Asadabad, Afghanistan. I wanted to thank you for all that you have done for our modest little church. We have been blessed with a small church made of plywood and tin there at Camp Wright. My coworkers and I often pass out the Psalm 91 bandanas and the small cards that give the guys and gals that are traveling between the bases some comfort not only from the Lord but they also let us know that we have not been forgotten back home."

Follow up email:

> "We scavenged some of the old buildings here on the FOB (Forward Operations Base) for two by fours and built pews. Operation Bandanas' program is one of the better received ones here. The bandanas are one of the fastest things that go out. Next are the music and candies and the passages we get that are laminated."

> "Many of these soldiers are young and on their first deployment. I think that these bandanas are an awesome reminder of God's love for them."

> "I have 5 FOBs I visit in E. Afghanistan, so I'll distribute the bandanas as I travel. Your prayers are appreciated for my fellow warriors who have it harder and are living in dangerous areas. Lord, keep blessing this ministry!" CH(CPT) Steve Satterfield, Jalalabad, Afghanistan

> "I just wanted to say thank you for the Psalm 91 bandana. Our Squadron received a package of bandanas. I will read it and carry it with me daily. Thank you for the constant reminder of God's love and thank you for making a difference in my life!" Bagram, Afghanistan

Our deployed troops face many fears on a daily basis, but they go out courageously day after day, night after night, because they know that freedom is more important than fear. They risk their lives for it. Our soldiers, sailors, airmen, and marines are worthy and deserving of our prayers, our thoughts, our time, our effort, and our resources.

> *"Courage is not the absence of fear, but rather the judgment that something else is more important than fear."*
> Ambrose Redmon

CHAPTER 9

Spiritual Fitness

The Army has developed a program called Comprehensive Soldier Fitness. Its purpose is "identifying individual shortfalls in five critical areas that comprise the total soldier: physical, emotional, social, family and spiritual" and "to build the resilience and enhance the performance of every soldier, family member, and DA (Department of the Army) civilian"(csf.army.mil). I feel that Operation Bandanas is helping respond to the comprehensive fitness of our soldiers by providing an item to aid in their spiritual fitness. I think that our mission can also help meet the needs in the other four areas. Psalm 91 is filled with words of comfort, strength, and courage; and eight wonderful promises of God. God can bring healing to the body and mind, strengthen families, and mend broken relationships.

How have so many helped meet this critical area of spiritual fitness and how can *you* help?

Our primary source of providing so many bandanas has been through churches from all across North America, the body of Christ, who have promoted the ministry in their church and then sent donations to Operation Bandanas to spiritually support our chaplains and soldiers, sailors, airmen and marine.

Women's missions organizations from a number of different denominations have done a phenomenal job in promoting our mission to their churches. When these ladies get involved, things start happening!

Operation Bandanas recently heard from a church that had one of their own deploying. They took up a collection to provide 225 bandanas personally for him and his unit. Another church provided 800 for a chaplain who was a member of their congregation and about to deploy.

Those living in a military community or have a National Guard Armory have provided the bandanas for a particular unit about to deploy. They have gotten the name of a chaplain they could bless with a gift of Psalm 91 bandanas to distribute to his troops. State National Guard and Reserve units quietly slip away from armories all across the U.S. as they are being called up more and more to supplement our over-extended active duty soldiers. All that needs to be done to support them is go to your State National Guard website.

Memorial and Honor gifts: A gift was given in memory of someone's dad who had recently passed away. He had served in the military himself many years ago, and his daughter wanted to remember him by supporting others who followed in her dad's footsteps of service. Another veteran was honored by his children on his 80th birthday with an honorarium given in his name. What a thoughtful gift!

Churches have planned and promoted patriotic events around Memorial Day, July 4th, and Veterans Day and taken an offering for Operation Bandanas in honor of those who are have served and are serving and in memory of those who have given their lives in service to their country.

Churches have given gifts of thanks specifically during the Thanksgiving season and expressions of love in February. We had one church do a "March for the Troops" during the month of March. I thought that was very clever!

Groups putting together goody boxes to send overseas purchased bandanas to enclose in them. They will not only be sending perishable items, but the imperishable food of God's Word, the bread of life.

Rather than asking for one bandana for one person, it is important to keep in mind their battle buddies also. Many soldiers would not receive a Psalm 91 bandana as a gift of encouragement and inspiration if not for the body of Christ assuring they receive them. And when one soldier gets a Psalm 91 bandana, he usually would like extras to share with his battle buddies.

A group of West Point parents in Texas purchased the bandanas for their sons' platoons (letter in chapter, Miraculous Deliverances). They have now passed information about our mission on to others, and we are getting contacted from their sharing. Word of mouth has been an amazing way for getting more people across the U.S. informed and involved. Email address books have been a great tool. Many have spread the word about this mission to others in their community through churches, organizations, and individuals by directing them to our website, which inspires them to get involved.

Youth, children, Sunday school/Bible classes, Vacation Bible Schools, Missions Organizations, Men's and Women's Ministries, 4-H, Scouts, etc., have adopted Operation Bandanas as a project.

Christian schools have promoted and supported our ministry. One Christian school does a yearly fundraiser to provide bandanas for an entire Battalion (600-800 troops). This is a great reminder to our young people of the sacrifices being made on their behalf (see chapter, Teaching Patriotism to the Next Generation).

Individual Sunday school classes, discipleship groups, and circles have contributed *ongoing* donations.

Individual donors are personally giving ongoing/monthly gifts either online through our website or by sending checks.

I speak personally to churches and organizations as time and distance permit in addition to displaying at conferences. Since I can't be all over the country at once, Operation Bandanas recorded a DVD with several different clips to choose from that have inspired many to get involved. It has been a great promotional tool. With the DVD, I actually *have* been all over the country!

We always need people to keep our mission, our military, our veterans, and their families in their prayers.

Encouraging our military during times of war should be a high priority of every American. Our soldiers presently on the battle front in Iraq and Afghanistan are weary and are being stretched physically, emotionally, and spiritually; as are their families. They need to know that they are respected, remembered, and appreciated.

To the churches and missions organizations throughout North Carolina and all across America who have supported this ministry, a heartfelt thanks. Your combined gifts have provided tens of thousands of bandanas. To those wonderful individuals who have sent personal gifts, you have made a big difference. Your generosity has touched and impacted lives in ways you'll never know! To those individuals who have been "that one person" who carried our ministry to their church and to other churches in their area who then adopted Operation Bandanas as one of their projects, you have been a personal blessing to many of our troops. The ripple effect that you were responsible for has been huge! To all the incredible volunteers of all ages who have packaged the bandanas, then prayed over each one, you have been a God send. Your loving touch, effort, and time are so appreciated-- not only by me, but by every serviceman or woman who receives a Psalm 91 bandana with your fingerprints on it. All of you have invested your resources and your time to tHIS mission. It takes an army of volunteers and generous individuals working together to keep sending Psalm 91 bandanas to our troops. Many thanks, precious friends, for lovin' our troops through the ministry of Operation Bandanas. This is your story too!

"I look upon the spiritual life of the soldier as even more important than his physical equipment. The soldier's heart, the soldier's spirit, the soldier's soul are everything. Unless the soldier's soul sustains him, he cannot be relied upon and will fail himself, his commander, and his country in the end. It's morale, and I mean morale, which wins the victory in the ultimate, and that type of morale can only come out of the religious fervor in his soul. I count heavily on that type of man and that type of Army."
General George C. Marshall

Good News from the Front

CH "Ike" in Kuwait

Baptism at JSS Doura

From the Front

"Thank you for the bandana. Sometimes churches send out stuff hoping it hits the mark, but never knowing. In this case, on a small forward base on the edge of Afghanistan, you did." FOB Salerno

"I just wanted to take a minute of your time to say thank you for the Psalm 91 bandana. I am a civilian contractor who is embedded with the 82nd Airborne in SW Afghanistan. I went to my first service in several months tonight and as I laid the Bible down after the service, I noticed the bandana. It will be washed and carried in my pocket everyday!"

"Today I received a bandana with an inspirational message on it from you. Thank you so much for taking the time to put together such a nice gift. It really means a lot. Sometimes it gets lonely out here and we feel like our friends and family forget about us. A nice gift like this helps remind us that we are not forgotten. Once again, thank you." Bagram, Afghanistan

"We handed out your bandanas at our Bible Study. I am an F-16 pilot flying out of Bagram Air Field, Afghanistan.

I plan to wear the bandana under my helmet as I fly in support of the Army guys on patrol. My wingman is also a Christian, which means we can pray together before our flights. Thanks again for all of your support. It really means a lot, and these bandanas are a great way to share God's love and strength." LTC HR, "Riddler"

"I was recently in the field for a week and endured 115 degree and more heat index. I brought your bandana with me. It was not only comfort to my head and face when I wiped it dry, but it was inspiration to my soul as I contemplated the meaning of Psalm 91. It is so fitting for us soldiers. Thank you for your prayers and your kindness. Honored to serve Americans like you." SPC Del Rosario

"I came across one of your bandanas in the Chaplain's office and I wanted to thank you. Thank you for the support, thank you for your prayers, and thank you for this bandana. We lost two more soldiers last week. Please consider their families and friends in your thoughts as we move forward without them. It's hot, I work long hours on guard duty, and I'm grateful to have this bandana." SPC CN

"I am a pilot with the U.S. Air Force currently deployed to Kandahar, Afghanistan and was recently sent one of your bandanas by a family friend. I found this to be a wonderful surprise and an inspiration as well. As I read Psalm 91, I am reminded of God's love for all of us and how that love is spread to others by people like you and your organization. It gives me great comfort as I carry the bandana with me knowing He is watching over and protecting all of us here. I just wanted to say thank you for remembering all of those folks over here serving the greatest nation on earth. It is because of people like you that inspire us to do what we do." Capt JP

"We are incredibly grateful for the bandanas. I can't keep them on hand. What a blessing you and your compadres are to us. I am amazed at all the troopers that are actively looking for the bandanas when we come around with them. Thank you! Please pass this on to those that are working with you on this. Thanks for being a ministry multiplier." CH(MAJ) Larry Pundt

"I wanted to take the opportunity to thank you for your support. I picked up one of your bandanas at a chaplain's building on Bagram Airfield, Afghanistan. It can get very lonely out here and it can be difficult when family back home is going through trials and I cannot be there physically to support them. It is a comfort to know God is there to be their fortress even when I cannot. The bandana was a great reminder of that and also amazingly practical as the weather gets hotter. Now I always have Psalm 91 to wipe the sweat and the troubles away. Again, I share my heartfelt thanks for your support. God Bless." Brian Kester, 1stLt, USAF

"In the name of our battalion, Combat Logistics Battalion 22, I would like to thank you for your thoughtfulness and assistance as you provided us with Psalm 91 bandanas to be distributed among the members of our command. Your prayers on behalf of our active duty Marines and Sailors are greatly appreciated as well. Trainings to accomplish physical and mental readiness are arduous and quite challenging. Your prayers and particularly the bandanas you sent us will help us to work on the spiritual readiness of our command in order to face the upcoming challenges of deployment.

I have shared your name with other chaplain friends. They may be contacting you for their battalions. Many of our Marines and Sailors have great memories of the bandanas from Iraq and Afghanistan. They used them there and felt God's protection as they put their lives on the line to serve our country. In the name of our battalion, I pray to the Lord for many blessings upon all of you that your ministry of love and prayers may continue touching the lives of all our military forces and turning them to the only fountain of life, hope and happiness." Semper Fidelis, Chaplain Diego Londono

"I want to send a special Thank You to you and the whole "Operation Bandanas" organization for the wonderful gift of 91st Psalm Bandanas that you have provided the 82nd Sustainment Brigade. Over the past month we sent off 100 Soldiers to Iraq and Afghanistan with the Bandanas and we will be sending off another 200 before the end of March. The Soldiers were excited and very grateful to receive them. As one of the Soldiers was getting on the bus yesterday after receiving his bandana, he said, "Thanks Chaplain, now I can always remember God's protection and presence with me." And that is exactly what you are helping our Soldier to do- to feel and know God's protection and care every moment of everyday. As St. Paul says, nothing in this world can separate us from God's love, and your gift helps our Soldiers to remember this. With Gratitude" Chaplain(CPT) Lauren Nofsinger

CH(CPT) Nofsinger handing out Ps 91 bandanas as soldiers board the bus for Green Ramp (the terminal where the troops from Ft. Bragg fly in and out of).

CHAPTER 12

Valuable Volunteers

No organization, particularly non-profits, could function without volunteers! I am so grateful to those who faithfully serve our troops through their time and energy. I have churches all over the community of Fayetteville, throughout the State of North Carolina and beyond, of all denominations, who assist Operation Bandanas in this effort. More and more churches that send donations want the bandanas to come back to them to carry it all the way through to the folding and packaging. They return the bandanas to me to mail to those on my list; mail to a unit they want to bless personally; or get an address from me of where to mail them.

These are just a few pictures of volunteers lovingly preparing the bandanas before sending them on to our troops. You can see they are all ages. Once finished, they lay their hands on the bandanas and pray over each one. It has taken a lot of hands to fold every bandana we have mailed, delivered, or had picked up. It's a true labor of love and becomes a great time of fellowship also.

Below is part of an email that I received from a chaplain to all who have, literally, put their hands into our ministry. Be encouraged for what you have done and continue to do for our troops and for Christ in your special part of tHIS ministry.

> "It's not only the bandanas but also the hands that fold the bandanas, the thoughts and prayers in the bandanas ministry that keep us comfortable."

Something "extra special":

> "I am a Minnesota National Guard Soldier currently stationed in Joint Base Balad, Iraq....I love the message printed on the bandana. Hope, faith and encouragement have never been so easy to carry! It is people like your group that make year-long deployments away from family and friends so much easier. Thank you for your time, efforts, and endless generosity. God bless you and your families." Lynette Hoke, SGT, MNARNG

> "P.S. There is something that makes the bandanas you give extra special...thank you again for blessing the troops." (Could it be the love and prayers put into each bandana we send??)

Hands On!

So Faithful!

*Children from First Baptist Church, Lumberton, North
Carolina, during a summer mission's camp.*

Girl Scouts at work!

Students giving their time.

Bible study sisters and wives of soldiers

CHAPTER 13

Teaching Patriotism to the Next Generation

17 July 2011

Dear Mary,

I hope you are well. I pray also that your ministry with Operation Bandanas is continuing to flourish.

The students at GRACE Christian School so enjoyed working on the bandana project. Each student in our kindergarten through sixth grade was able to decorate a card that would be enclosed with a bandana. Our Student Council held a special work session to fold and stuff the baggies. It was an exciting time!

When our parents came for our awards ceremony we dedicated all the bandanas. We presented a bandana to one of our school dads who is a recruiter with the U.S. Navy. He then stood in place as we prayed for the bandanas and their prayer cards to reach the military personnel safely and for the men and women who serve our country. It would have touched your heart to hear these young children praying so sincerely for our country and our military.

Thank you so much for giving us the opportunity to join with you in this wonderful ministry. Our school strives to teach patriotism and we are very involved in community and mission outreach projects, so your project was a perfect fit for us.

We wish you the best with your ministry. Thank you for the time, energy, and efforts you have put into this ministry. We pray for a continued fruitful outreach as you minister to our United States Military.

Sincerely,
Kathie Thompson
K-6 Principal
GRACE Christian School
Raleigh, NC

It is important for our children and youth to be sensitized to the extraordinary service of our men and women serving our nation in uniform. I am thankful that this school and others like it are teaching patriotism. Schools teach American history lessons and world history lessons about the patriots of the Revolutionary War, the cost of the Civil War, the heroes of WWI and WWII, and so on. Our soldiers, sailors, airmen and marines are making history today. They are the present day, real life patriots and heroes. They are fighting for the future of our nation and our children and youth who are living this part of history. Our troops go to battle so that perhaps their own children and the next generation will not have to. Let us teach our young people gratitude for their service.

Students at Village Christian Academy in Fayetteville, NC, raised money to supply CH(CPT) Marshall Cohen with Ps 91 bandanas for his battalion's upcoming deployment. Mrs. Montouth, on the left, was the Middle School Principal at that time. It has become an annual event for VCA to promote Operation Bandanas to provide bandanas to our troops. CH Cohen's battalion commander had two students enrolled at the school and saw the bandana on display in the Middle School Office. He asked how he could get them for all 800 of his soldiers, and VCA and Operation Bandanas took it from there! The testimonies of the battalion commander, LTC Brunson, and Chaplain Cohen are on our DVD.

Here are some quotes from Chaplain Cohen before he prayed with the students:

> "How many of you have been to camp and have a T-shirt to remember it by? The T-shirt reminds you of how God was with you and allowed you to grow and bless you that weekend or at that event. These bandanas, for a lot of our soldiers, are those T-shirts. They'll put the bandana on and know how God is with them and moving in their lives. So I want to encourage you that as you are in prayer for us and you see these bandanas, they are not just a bandana; they are so much more. Your prayers are more important to us than anything else will ever be, but these bandanas are our T-shirts when we are far, far away from our homes, our children, and our loved ones, and we can look and know that you guys had an integral part in how God is moving in the lives of our soldiers and leaders."

Michael Brown on left with Noah and Benjamin Gray (two of my grandsons!)

CHAPTER 14

Dear Hero

Notes Enclosed with Bandanas from Children and Youth

"Dear Hero,

All I can say is thank you! You keep our whole country safe; that is quite an amazing feat. Everyone here in America is in debt to all that you have done. The verse on the bandana is Psalm 91 and in my opinion, one of the best in the world!! If you ever feel alone, read the verse and know that you are safe at all times. Everyone here is praying for you guys. xoxoxo"

Larysa
"PS God loves you!"

"YOU ROCK!"

"Stay strong because before you know it, you'll be home."
From Hailey

"Thank you for all you do for America. You truly are a hero. God is the ultimate Hero and He will protect you as you serve this great country. People like you protect average people like me who don't know what it means to be a soldier. Once again, I thank you for all you do for me and my family and for all the other people in America." Sincerely, Alex

"I hope your [sic] OK wherever you are, and I wish you have everything you need. God bless you." Tyjiana

"You encourage me by your service. Thank you."

"You may not feel like it but you are a big part of our country. Your bravery has helped us. Thank you for serving our country." Love, Ally

"You should feel protected, but powerful, because God is by your side."

"Thank you for serving our country and fighting for freedom." Everett

"Thanks for giving up all your freedom and family time for the freedom of our country. I will pray for you"

"I would like to take the time to thank you for your sacrifices to fight for our freedom. I understand how hard it would be to leave your family because my dad is in the military and he had to serve overseas for what seemed like an eternity. May God bless you and keep you safe. I hope you enjoy this bandana." Mary Cate

"Just because you fight, we are FREE. Thank you for all that you do!"

"Shine like the sun and be the brave soldier I know you are."

"Be strong and of good courage; be not frightened; neither be dismayed; for the Lord your God is with you wherever you go." Joshua 1:9

"Just a note, that's all I give, but you give so much. Thank you for everything you do."

"To a Hero,

Thank you for serving our country to keep us safe and protect America. May God guide you and have His way in your life. May He direct your paths so if you get lost, He can guide you to Him. Thank you for everything that you do and keep doing your duty." Love, Lauren

"My name is Drew. I wish you safety on your service overseize [sic]. We pray every day at our school for the troops that God be with them. I thank you for everything you have done for our country and our freedom. May God be with you all." Drew

"I just wanted to let you know that I am so thankful for everything you do and all the sacrifices you make. Never feel scared or alone because I and many other people are praying for you and your protection. Keep on trusting that

God will take care of you no matter what. Once again, thank you for everything." Kelsia

"Thank you for taking time to fight for our country. I am thinking about you and praying for you. Be safe!" Love, Anna Grace

"We thank you for protecting our country and families. I'm also grateful for you sacrificing your time, family and life to protect us. We hope you'll enjoy our bandanas." Sincerely, Lee

"We love you for saving our country and sacrificing your lives." Love, Scotty

"I can do all things through Christ who strengthens me. Philippians 4:13. Thank you!"

"Thank you so much for serving in the war. I hope that you are all safe and will come home soon. Thank you for being brave enough to step up and fight in the war so people here in America can have their peace and freedom. I don't think anyone could do anything braver than what you are doing right now. I know how it feels to miss your family, but I think it feels worse being overseas. I think that is one of the ultimate sacrifices, leaving your friends and family to serve in the military. I don't think I'll ever be able to thank you enough for what you're doing, but I really do appreciate it. Thank you so much for being such a brave person." Love, Adrianna

"Thank you for protecting the country." From Michael, 3rd Grade

"Every night I pray that you will not be afraid to cross the battlefield. I do not know if you have a family but if you do bless them and you. I won't forget to pray for you. My name is Adrian D and I have faith in all of you."

"I personally wanted to thank you for all that you and your Army do for us. Your family must be proud of you and I am too. I am grateful to have you over there fighting for us. We love you and be safe! God bless you!" Love, Alice

"Thank you so very much for serving and protecting our country! I hope you make it home safe! God will always be there to protect you! We are constantly praying for you daily! Thank you." Ashley

"Thank you for everything you are doing for our country. Jesus will keep you safe in His arms. Freedom doesn't come free. I can't thank you enough for fighting for our freedom. May the Lord bless you and your loved ones. When you come back home, I pray that God will give you strength and rest. I hope you will come back soon so that you can see your family and friends. Thank you again for keeping America safe." Love Courtney

"I really appreciate everything that you have sacrificed for me and my country. Your work and patriotism, among other things, has really inspired me to stand up for my country. I am praying for you and I hope this blesses you!" In Jesus, Katherine

"Jesus loves you and America does too." from Hailey

"Every day I pray that you will not get hurt or wounded. I hope that you'll love God and obey Him every day!" Love, Tiffany

"I'm proud to be an American because you make me free."

"When I grow up, I will always remember that you have given up everything for my protection."

"You keep us safe while risking your life and giving up time with your family. You deserve more than a card."

"Hi! My name is Ryan and I wanted to send you a bandana. This verse is a very powerful and moving one. God cares about everyone so much. He made the birds and the plants and everything you see around you. But His most important creation was us. Even when you are out in the fight, maybe with bullets flying around, God is there with you. He is beside you when you need someone. God will never let you down and He will never leave you. Everyone back home at my school is praying for you. We all believe that you are fighting for our freedom and from everyone here, I'd like to say thank you for protecting us."

"You are an awesome person. Thanks so much. I have no words to describe how much I THANK YOU!"

"Keep going. You can do it! And thank you!"

"Thank you sooo much for all you do. I appreciate how much effort, courage, and bravery that you have put forth in order to keep America safe and free! Thanks for all that you have done for our country. Please always remember that God loves you and you are His beloved son/daughter. He loves you sooo much. Thanks for all you do! Ashley

"Trust in the Lord and He will save you from any harm, because you are His child."

"Thank you for what you have done. Every last one of you is a miracle to all of us. God bless you!"

"You are a big hearted person! Thanks for everything you do!"

"We pray and cheer you on and thank you for all your hard work. We love you."

"Thank you SO much for serving our country. We are so blessed to have soldiers like you who would freely give their lives for our country. Remember ALWAYS that we are praying for you and that we are so thankful. God bless!"Katie

"I want to thank you for risking your life for mine. Thank you for leaving your family, your friends and your comfort zone so I can stay in mine. I am in debt to you. I know what it feels like to be away from family but I don't know what it feels like to be away and overseas. My father is in the military and overseas, I can relate to your family members who miss you so much. So as you hold this bandana, remember how much you are appreciated and loved. More importantly, GOD loves you and He wants the best for you. Don't ever give up or think it's useless."

"You are Brave. You are True.
Thanks for Fighting. I love you."

Writing notes.

Thank you for all that you are doing to ensure freedom at home and around the world. May this Psalm 91 Bandana bring you encouragement, comfort, strength and inspiration. God bless, cover and protect you with a piece of His armor (Ephesians 6:10-17). You are in our prayers.

WE LOVE YOU GUYS!

Given to you through Operation Bandanas for Bragg from grateful and generous citizens and friends, churches, businesses, organizations, and families of our military.

OPERATION BANDANAS FOR BRAGG
c/o Mary Gray
PO Box 9550 • Fayetteville, NC 28311
bandanas91@yahoo.com
www.braggbandanas.org

Personalized cards.

Thank you for all that you are doing to ensure freedom at home and around the world. May this Psalm 91 Bandana bring you encouragement, comfort, strength and inspiration. God bless, cover and protect you with a piece of His armor (Ephesians 6:10-17). You are in our prayers.

WE LOVE YOU GUYS!

Given to you through Operation Bandanas for Bragg from grateful and generous citizens and friends, churches, businesses, organizations, and families of our military.

OPERATION BANDANAS FOR BRAGG
c/o Mary Gray
PO Box 9550 • Fayetteville, NC 28311
bandanas91@yahoo.com
www.braggbandanas.org

From
Hailey

Stay strong because before you know it you'll be home.

WELCOME
HOME

Personalized cards.

CHAPTER 15

Miraculous Deliverances

From Chaplain Rod Gilliam:

"In 2007-2008, I was with an Infantry unit in Baghdad. It was with the 2-325, 2BCT, 82nd ABN. Your organization sent us several hundred bandanas. They were a very popular item. There was one NCO that would read Psalm 91 from his bandana every time he went outside the wire (for you civilians reading this, a term used when leaving the safety of the compound). It got to the point that he memorized it and would quote it to his team every time they departed. He was hit by an IED that exploded his vehicle. No one was hurt. The following Sunday that soldier was in my chapel. I had him start the service by quoting Psalm 91. It was powerful.

There was another Soldier wearing the bandana that was shot in his Kevlar helmet by a sniper in the forehead area. The round mysteriously tumbled on the inside of the helmet and exited a clean hole through the rear of the helmet. Amazingly, the Soldier was unscratched (with a bullet hole through the front and back of his helmet!) He came to my chapel service that evening and testified. He said, 'It's been several years since I have been to church but if I don't come now and give God the glory, I don't know what it's going to take to wake me up!' The Soldier recommitted his life to Christ that evening. These are just two of the incredible stories down range that your organization was a part of. I thank you for it."

This is an email I received in August, 2010, from Dottie Jones, a mom in Dallas, Texas, who made sure that her son--a West Point graduate, and at the time of this email, an infantry platoon leader--was provided enough Psalm 91 bandanas to cover him and his platoon of soldiers. She also got other parents of West Point graduates involved in getting the bandanas for their sons' platoons. This is an amazing account of what these young soldiers encountered on four incredibly perilous days:

> "Doug never leaves his tent without his bandana and by all rights, short of miracles he has seen, he and half his platoon should be dead. Doug and his platoon were in a 96 hour battle on the border of Pakistan where 150 Taliban were killed, some within 20 yards of them. While evacuating the last of several injured soldiers off the mountainside, and after very little sleep in 110 degree weather with most everyone de-hydrated and throwing up, Doug went back up the mountain to carry the last man down on his back. While doing so an RPG (Rocket Propelled Grenade) grazed the side of his leg without exploding. He told us that was where he was carrying his bandana that day. He and his men were able to get the injured soldiers on the Medivac helicopter while under intense fire without any American casualties.
>
> Afterwards, he and his platoon gathered in a hut for prayer and while looking around noticed that several men had bullet holes in their sleeves but were unharmed. The newest member of his platoon would have been killed by a bullet to the chest but his ammo canteen stopped it from killing him. He said what they have seen in the way of miracles, gives the miracle of water to wine a run for its money. (Spoken with all due respect.) He asked us to tell

everyone who is praying (and I know you are) thank you
and to please keep holding them up in prayer daily."

Try to envision this battle these young soldiers experienced. Think of
the physical condition that they were in, dehydrated and throwing up, little
sleep, little time to eat whatever meager rations they had, stressed, scared,
exhausted, hot, yet, they had to keep on fighting for their lives and for the
lives of their battle buddies. Thank God right now for the extraordinary
courage, stamina, and determination of young men like this whose lives
are literally on the front line of defense for us. They are young Americans
who have gone to the fight and have willingly volunteered to face any enemy
that comes against them and comes against our nation. They are our real
American heroes...not the ones we read about on the sports pages or in
the entertainment section of newspapers and magazines. Remember these
young patriots and their families in your prayers. Never forget.

CHAPTER 16

My Hero
Author Unknown

I received this via email several years ago close to a Super Bowl Sunday. I have scoured the internet to try to determine who the author is, but to no avail. Whoever wrote it is a genius!

My hero wore a helmet too. It wasn't a gleaming helmet with a team symbol on the side, though. It was covered in a camouflage pattern and bore the marks of the months of use it had seen.

The dirt on my hero's face didn't come from a field of grass in a stadium in America. It came from streets and foxholes in a far off land.

My hero didn't have a ball zinged past him. Instead, he felt hot lead whistle past his head and shrapnel rip at his clothes.

When the skirmish subsided, my hero didn't get doused with Gatorade and head to a hot shower. Instead, he collapsed, exhausted, next to the wheel of a truck, hands shaking from what he had just experienced.

He didn't get any cell phone calls congratulating him on a big win. Instead, he shook the hand of his buddy and thanked God they both had survived.

My hero didn't get a shiny trophy or a ring or a million dollar contract extension. My hero got the satisfaction of knowing that he had made a difference for freedom and liberty in a way most will never know.

My hero didn't lay down the ball after four quarters. My hero fought the fight until he laid down his life.

Today, there are men and women in places around the world, wearing a uniform with the Stars and Stripes on their shoulder, who are REAL heroes. Their stories won't make the front page, they won't be talked about in every restaurant and bar in town. But their impact on the life that you and I know will far surpass that of the sports figures that will get the attention.

I hope we, as a society, can keep it all in perspective.

One of our helmeted heroes

CHAPTER 17

From the Front

"This is my 3rd tour, 2 years in Iraq and now here in Afghanistan. My job, much to my wife's disliking, is to hunt IED's (Improvised Explosive Devices) and their makers/emplacers. Our unit travels the roads everyday and searches them out. It is, as you can imagine, a dangerous job. I have been carrying this bandana for some time now. I had two, but used one to patch up a kid's arm and thought he needed it worse than I did. I read it each time we head out and carry it on each and every mission."

"Your bandanas mean a lot to all of our Marines here at VMM-261. We are blessed to have people like you and your organization who are willing to take time out of their busy lives to put a smile on a young Marine's face. This day in age people like you and Operation Bandanas are few and far between. Your kindness and generosity serve as a reminder of what exactly it is that we are fighting for. Our Marines are proud to serve and each of them is here of their own free will, readily putting themselves in harm's way so that our great nation can remain free." David W. Lewis, Captain, USMC, VMM-261 Morale Officer

"I am currently training at one of my pre-mobilization installations with the 20th Special Forces Group (Airborne). I just wanted to take a few moments to express my gratitude for the service and the prayers that you provide our troops. I love paratrooping, and I am more than sure that I speak for everyone within my section and say that when we jump into our Drop Zones (combat ready or not) we are forever grateful to have our Psalm 91 bandanas. I experienced a near fatal car accident a couple of years ago... crushed my ankle, knee and broke my femur, went through physical therapy and now tie my Psalm 91 bandana around my right knee every time I jump. Your gesture is a total blessing!" SPC Zachary Maldonado

"Thank you for the Psalm 91 bandana. I have it hanging in my conex housing unit and I read all or part of it every day. I am a Bible believer so I did not want to get the beautiful bandana dirty wearing it. It inspires me daily. Thank you again. May the Lord bless you in your ministry." 1st SGT MM, Kabul, Afghanistan

"I want to thank you for the bandanas to our troops. They were a real hit. On a practical level many of the Soldiers took them and were using them to wear on their head before putting on the helmet. It helped keep the sweat off their brow in the incredible heat. I was having a problem for awhile with soldiers hoarding them. We are on a combat outpost where supplies can be limited at times so when something of value comes in, people tend to grab them up quickly.

On a spiritual note, it was good to get the Psalm 91 chapter out to so many Soldiers with such a variety of beliefs and backgrounds. For some, it was probably the first time they have ever heard the passage that we as Christians cherish in times of danger or duress. For many of us as believers, Psalm 91 will always be a section of scripture that we will always look to for strength and comfort. Having it on a bandana is just one more way to keep the truth of the promise in front of us."

"Hello there from Farah, Afghanistan. We are an Army National Guard unit from AZ. I was walking by the soldiers table at mail call and I picked up your little gift bag which had your note in it. Just wanted to, on behalf of my squad and PLT, thank you for all that you do for us soldiers. It means a lot. We will proudly wear them." SSG WR

"I wanted to say thank you for your prayers and your support. The bandanas are a wonderful blessing for our paratroopers. In our unique mission and location, our troopers battle with the wind and dust almost on a daily basis. The bandanas work wonders, and the troops love them! When out on mission, it's not uncommon at all for me to see soldiers either wearing them under their helmets or carrying one in their hand. It's a great practical blessing, but moreover it's an excellent spiritual blessing. Not only are our fellow brothers and sisters in Christ encouraged by it, but it has afforded me another platform to share the gospel. I am excited to see how God will use your faithfulness through these bandanas to advance His kingdom." For Him...CH (CPT) Jeff Smith, Iraq

With their bandanas.

CHAPTER 18

The Kid, the Bandana and a Super Bowl

A Journal entry received from SFC Dennis Mitchell
3 February 2008

I try and title these with some relevance to what it's about. I've wanted to write about our youngest Soldier for some time and just hadn't got around to it yet. There were a series of events that took place today that make this a neat and tidy little story.

There are certain things that I always make sure I carry with me on patrol. One is a small US flag and the other is an old Desert pattern bandana. I carry them both in my upper left breast pocket close to my heart. The flag I received in Bangor, Maine, before flying over here the last time. The bandana I received in 1999 when I came over to Kuwait for a six month tour. The bandana has Psalm 91 printed on it. Psalm 91 is a verse that discusses God our protector on it.

For those that know me know I rarely go to church but they also know I have strong Christian values and beliefs. If I could find a bandana with Psalm 57 or Psalm 35 on them I would probably carry it instead. So what does a bandana with Psalm 91 on it have to do with the kid and the Super Bowl?? Glad you asked.

Kyle Welch is our youngest Soldier in the platoon and comes to us from the Great State of Ohio. He was born on December 13th, 1988. PFC Welch came to us in early November but wasn't allowed to deploy with us until early January so he could complete mandatory training. PFC Welch had left his laptop out and some of the Soldiers decided to snoop on it. They found a video of PFC Welch in dress uniform giving testimony to the Hamilton Church of God congregation taken sometime in December. The soldiers laughed about how goofy this young soldier looked and wanted to give him a hard time later about it. I scolded the Soldiers for invading someone else's privacy and felt I had found a candidate to pass my bandana to. I took out my neatly folded bandana and placed it on Welch's bunk. I never said anything to him about it but knew he'd figure out what to do with it.

After our patrol briefs there is a Chaplain that gives us a short prayer before we roll out. I had asked him if he had seen the Psalm 91 bandanas and if so if he knew where I could get one. He knew exactly what I was talking about. He said he knew a lady named Mary that may be able to get them for us. Good enough for me so we have now tied a bandana and a young Soldier together. Where does the Super Bowl come into all of this??? Glad you asked!!

We had an early patrol scheduled for the evening that the Super Bowl would be played. We all hoped we would be back before it started so we could watch it. We had work to do and the area we would be doing Route Clearance is our worst...Sadr City. When I walked in for our patrol brief the Chaplain informed me that he had something for us. He had received the Psalm 91 bandanas with the new ACU pattern. The brief was finished and the Chaplain came up to the front of the room and read us Psalm 91. He then offered the bandanas to who ever wanted one. I quickly took one and walked over to PFC Welch. *"Can I have mine back now?"* I said to him. I explained to the young Soldier the importance of it to me and handed him a new one. He looked at me with a puzzled look finally figuring out who had left a bandana on his bunk a month earlier. As I figured, he pulled my old desert pattern bandana out of his pocket and handed it back.

The patrol is going well but there is a certain level of nervousness when we approach Sadr City. I called the Patrol Leader over the radio and recommended we arrange our patrol into a more defensive formation. I can't explain what a defensive formation is but basically we arrange our weapons systems and vehicles in a manner to provide the best protection. The Patrol Leader has me contact the unit that is responsible for the area we are going into. I call up the Platoon that has observation posts in the area. *"Comanche 1-6 this is Comanche*

Iron claw 4-7 entering your battle space with seven victors and 23 souls. Request status in the area."…" "4-7 this is 1-6…we've been waiting for you guys. Let your guys know that they will probably take fire when they pass the intersection of Delta and Gold." "Roger...I'll let 'em know." "Don't worry we got your backside. We'll be shadowing you throughout the whole route." I let the guys know and we prepared as we approached Delta and Gold for a possible ambush.

Now I have to let you know that small arms fire on the vehicles we have is useless for the enemy to use. It's more an annoyance or harassment but it still can raise your heartbeat. The first four vehicles pass the intersection with nothing then suddenly all hell breaks loose.

Our third vehicle takes a single shot from our 2 o'clock position from about 100 meters away. The enemy is trying to make us focus all our attention at the 2 o'clock so that they can flank us with automatic weapons fire but no one bites. Suddenly it opens up on our 9 o'clock from a window less than 50 meters away. My gunner yells out in a strong Columbian accent, *"I see them Sergeant…there's two guys on the roof shooting at us and one in the window. They're shooting at us Sergeant!"* The vehicle in front of us starts to open up with their .50 caliber machine gun. *"Well why don't you shoot back dumbass!"* I quickly tell him. *"Roger Sergeant!"* You can hear the ting-ting-ting sound of rounds off the gunner's shield of our vehicle from the insurgents as my gunner starts to engage.

There is no sound quite like a .50 caliber machine gun especially in an urban environment where the sounds of gunfire echo off 3-4 story buildings. It gets your adrenaline going and from where I sit I can tell the gunner in front of me and my gunner is giving 'em hell. They quickly fire off around 50-60 rounds each before the shadow unit begins to engage. *"4-7 this is 1-6 we got it now"* and we continue our mission. I can see two insurgents jumping from roof to roof trying to escape the gunfire from the vehicles shadowing us.

As we're finishing up our patrol I'm wondering who was on the gun in front of us. I assume it was one of our more seasoned Soldiers because whoever it was rocked that gun with precision fire like there was no tomorrow. I was pleasantly surprised when I found out that it was PFC Kyle Welch.

We made it back in time to watch the last half of a very exciting Super Bowl. Not only did the New York Giants win the Lombardi Trophy as NFL champs but the two youngest Soldiers of the Platoon earned their Combat

Action Badges that they will display with pride when they return home on leave. They will take with them their own war story that I am sure they will share with their families and friends for years to come. The kid, the bandana and a Super Bowl!

6 February 2008 (three days after SFC Mitchell's journal entry, a note from the above mentioned chaplain that we sent the bandanas to.)

"Mary, just last night while I was at the convoy brief when I pray with them, one of the soldiers who was about to go "outside the wire" (with his Route Clearance Platoon, who search IED's, a very dangerous mission) asked me if I had any more bandanas, so I walked back to my Battalion to pick up some more and when other soldiers saw me carrying them, they came up to me wanting them also. The bandanas go like hot cakes! It's neat to hear that God has called you to do this. Thanks." CH Chris Carson

PFC Kyle Welch who earned his Combat Action Badge that night.

CHAPTER 19

Route Clearance

I have included another entry from SFC Dennis Mitchell's Journal. I asked him if I could share this with you because it's important that we always keep in mind how truly courageous our service men and women are. When you read, The Ambush Awaits, you'll know what I'm talking about. It gives us a small window into their experience. The courage and never quit attitude of these soldiers is almost beyond comprehension. Take your time reading it and try to imagine it. It's pretty descriptive. Route clearance is a very dangerous job. These soldiers risk their lives to clear the way to save other soldiers lives. Heroes...every one of them.

THE FIGHT FOR SADR CITY

Sadr City is 8 square miles of Shiite slums that has 2.5 million inhabitants. To understand the density of people that equates to 3200 people for every city block. Earlier this month the Mahdi militia conducted a series of brazen mortar attacks from the Southern edge of Sadr City using 107mm rockets aimed at the Green Zone. It seems that 107mm rockets have a range of 3.5 miles and the southern edge is right at 3 miles from the green zone. In one of these attacks three Americans were killed and 31 injured.

US forces have been on a mission for the last two weeks to push the militia out of this area. The line that was drawn was Route Gold which I mentioned earlier. That entry was about "The Kid, the Bandana and a Super Bowl." The plan is to emplace a Combat Outpost in this area and an Iraqi

Army outpost so that we have observation and limit activity. Towers and concrete T-walls are to be emplaced strategically to limit traffic flow and regulate activity. Route Clearance has been tasked to clear roads so barriers can be emplaced.

THE MISSION

For the past three days we have been conducting Route Clearance in support of this barrier mission. Our Route was Route Delta all the way to Route Gold. The plan is to clear with M1 Abrams tanks following closely as security and when we reached the intersection then the tanks would secure the intersection while barriers and towers were positioned. Because of the high probability of finding something, we had an Explosive Ordinance Team embedded with our team.

The first night was quiet but it seemed like everything that could go wrong did. We were unorganized and communication amongst the team stunk. Luckily it was uneventful. After we returned to COP Callahan I talked with my Platoon Leader about how the platoon will emulate whatever personality we have that evening. We talked about being better prepared and remaining patient.

The second night we did a detailed patrol brief and discussed what to do if all hell broke loose. On this night I could see men moving on the rooftops and was on edge. I called the tanks behind us *"Steel Blue this is Easy 1-7...we have two turds on the building to our nine...their hiding behind a tarp...we lost sight." "This is Steel Blue...we got it."* and we continued our clearance. As much as I would have loved to stay and engage the bad guys that wasn't our mission so we continued on. Suddenly I saw a group of men moving on the fourth floor roof approximately 200 meters away. *"Gunner...got 'em...switch to 7.62."* Just as he was about to engage, the figure moved its head to face us, and to my surprise I saw the perfect outline of a goat's head, floppy ears and all. *"It's a damn goat...why would there be goats on the fourth floor roof of a building...only in Iraq!!!"* The rest of the mission went smoothly as planned.

When we returned I again talked with the Platoon Leader about how much smoother things went when we just put a little preparation into the mission and good communication. He agreed and we vowed to make sure we got back to the basics of troop leading.

THE AMBUSH AWAITS, 11 APRIL 2008

The third night began just as the second with a thorough, detailed and complete Patrol brief conducted by the Patrol Leader and myself. We had established battle drills in case all hell had broken loose. We discussed actions on contact, medevac procedures, casualty evacuation and discussed everyone's responsibilities. On this night Comanche Iron Claw, another route clearance team, would be clearing a road 700 meters to our north on Route 'Bama.

The patrol started uneventfully when we suddenly hear an explosion to our north. Our Lieutenant calls out *"Comanche Iron Claw just struck an IED to our north. No injuries but their Husky is toast...we may have to clear our route and theirs."* I hate this area and the least amount of time in it the better I feel. *"We'll clear Route Delta, turn left on Gold, and then clear 'Bama from the north to south."*

To better understand, Route Delta is approximately a mile of Route Clearance and Bama runs the same direction a half mile to the north. This is not a huge route but it's littered with garbage and threats.

It's 10:51 at night when we make the left turn onto Route Gold. The Tanks have staged themselves at the intersection and we're traveling north to get to Bama. Within the first 100 meters we have the first IED strike. BOOM!!! It strikes our lead husky driven by SPC Jacob Janssen...*"I'm good, it struck early"* he quickly calls out over the radio. The Lieutenant calls out *"Let's keep pushing".* The IED was in the middle of the road directed at the opposite lane. The blast created a huge fireball but was too far off the road to cause any damage. Less than a minute later it happens again...BOOM!...again striking the lead Husky driven by Janssen...*"I'm good sir but it blew out a light"*...quickly the Lieutenant says *"Keep pushing".*

I'm calling up higher to let them know there is no damage and we were continuing our mission. In my mind I'm thinking about the sanity of this career choice. The second blast sent a piece of copper spall high in the air and was quite dramatic. Suddenly it happens again...BOOM!!!! Within a minute three IED's have detonated on our Route Clearance team. This time it narrowly passed by the backend of the Lieutenant's vehicle... *"We're good, keep pushing!"* The tanks that are watching are in total disbelief of how we keep pushing forward oblivious to anything but our mission.

My gunner and I are scanning the buildings with the Bradley Fighting Vehicle when I spot men moving in the fourth floor window of a six floor building. We open up on the window as the men try and move across the room. *"Okay...up...up...got 'em."* The Lieutenant is temporarily confused and comes across the radio *"Who's shooting?"* I let him know what we had and he tells everyone to be on the lookout for anyone moving around. "BOOM!!!" the lead Husky gets hit again. *"Sir...I have no lights but I'm good."* The Patrol Leader calmly says, *"Okay Husky two, switch with Husky one".* Husky two is being driven by CPL Stephen Defino and he quickly jumps into the lead.

I'm continuing to scan for men in the buildings and thinking *"this is insane!!!"* Everyone is as calm as a group of men playing cards. We've taken four IED strikes in a minute and a half but we're plugging away clearing the route just as we've been trained to do. Not a worry in the world but preparing for the next blast. As expected it happens again this time on CPL Defino's Husky. Boom!!!! The silence is unnerving as we wait to hear him come over the radio to announce he's good.

For what seemed like an eternity, others in the team were trying to determine if CPL Defino was okay. Though the radio is silent from CPL Defino's vehicle, there are small arms and Rocket Propelled Grenades that begin to rain down on our Route Clearance Team. One of the gunners, SPC Robert Themel, spots a man leaning over the roof to shoot a Rocket Propelled Grenade when he carefully places a three round burst of .50 caliber machine gunfire in the man's chest. Another gunner, Private Bent sweeps his machine gun fire through a second floor area and kills another man aiming down on the vulnerable team. For a split second everyone is firing like crazy and all I can think is *"This is kind of cool!"*

While this is happening another vehicle is positioning itself so that it can see if Defino's okay. When he pulls beside the struck vehicle he can see Defino agonizing in pain waving desperately for help. Our casualty evacuation drill that we had discussed in the brief suddenly kicked into high gear. Vehicles repositioned themselves to provide security so that Defino could be extracted.

While this is happening, two RPG's are fired and small arms continue to ping around the vehicles. M1 tanks move to provide security and my vehicle is opening up with main gun fire at the third floor of a building. We position our vehicle to receive Defino and wait for the word that security is set.

Suddenly tanks begin to fire their main gun and the noise is as loud as the IED blasts themselves. Confusion begins to set in but everyone remains calm. *"Security set!"* and we lower the ramp on our Bradley to evacuate Defino. The medic and SGT Eddie Doyle quickly exit the back of my vehicle as we begin firing at another group of men hiding in the building. I look at the hit husky and notice small arms fire all around the men trying to get Defino out of the Husky. This encourages us to fire more suppressive fire and the area is lit up with every vehicle around firing. The noise is deafening with explosions rocking everyone. I see that they have Defino out and we quickly get him loaded into our vehicle. Just before he is loaded into the vehicle there is a sudden explosion from the building we have been peppering the entire time and night turns to day as a fireball engulfs it. As we pull away popcorn sounds come from the building as the rounds from the insurgents cook off.

My job in the situation is casualty evacuation. Once there is a casualty I have to get the soldier to medical care as soon as possible. We pull away as the firefight is still going on to evacuate Defino. We get to a safe area and I open the door exposing where the Medic is treating Defino. Our medic is "Doc Fuqua" and he is cutting off Defino's clothes exposing wounds for treatment. Defino is moaning but seems okay. *"What we got Doc?"* He quickly calls out…*"He's got some burns and shrapnel in his backside."* There is the smell of blood and burning hair and flesh that emanate from the back of the vehicle but I can tell that Defino will fight another day. I continue to listen to the firefight as we take Defino to a medical facility. He is quickly stabilized and flown to start his recovery. CPL Defino received small copper fragments all along his lower back and buttocks. One of the frags did penetrate into his abdomen so he will have a long recovery.

I continue to be blown away with the bravery of these young men. I could not have been prouder of any of them. What gives a man the strength to drive on in the face of danger? We all knew when we made the turn on Route Gold that there was a high probability we could get blown up. After the second, then third and then fourth strike no one would have said anything if my Lieutenant would have aborted the mission. We already had three vehicles with damage but no one wavered. Without hesitation men dismounted to help Defino get out of the vehicle as small arms ricocheted all around them. I cannot find the words to describe what I witnessed from these fine young men.

When I returned to COP Callahan I had tons of paperwork to do. The Husky that CPL Defino was in was a total loss; awards had to be written and sworn statements done. The events of the evening were captured by a rooftop camera and our command confirmed we had 15 enemy KIA. My emotions were on a roller coaster from what I just witnessed and even though I should have been tired I couldn't sleep. I called CPL Defino's wife to update her on her husband and let her know he would be okay. I told her he was joking with us as we were riding along and gave her the series of events that were sure to follow. Almost twelve hours after the blast I sat on a bench quietly going through the events in my head over and over again. The emotions from the night's events filled my head until I couldn't hold it in anymore, and I quietly sat there and cried.

SFC Dennis A. Mitchell
E Co. 1-68 AR/ 3rd BDE/ 4ID
Unit# 6065 COP Callahan

SFC Dennis Mitchell

CHAPTER 20

Send Bandanas

We get requests for the Psalm 91 bandanas almost everyday...big requests... whole battalions at a time requests (500-800 soldiers). Early on in the ministry, I would receive numerous emails requesting the bandanas and worry how I'd be able to meet the requests. I would really get distressed because I knew that they wanted the bandanas ASAP. I would often have to tell them I would put them on my list and as donations were received, I would order bandanas for them. I knew they didn't want to be put on a list. And that really bothered me.

God reminded me one day that He would provide whatever was needed. I knew in my heart that He could and He would...so...I decided not to worry anymore! Worry is when we think we have to carry the burden ourselves. We forget all about our big God Who is our burden bearer and Who is quite capable of handling whatever it is we are worrying about. If you worry, you don't trust. But if you trust, you don't worry. My God has shown Himself trustworthy and faithful to me over and over and over. He would manage this ministry just fine! We can be at peace knowing He is our Jehovah Jireh, the God Who provides. (If you are a worrier, claim Philippians 4:6-7, my personal favorite, and Matthew 6:25-34.)

Here's a sample of some of those requests:

"I am the chaplain for the 115th Signal Battalion. Recently I received some bandanas from another chaplain to distribute and I was shocked at the response and requests for bandanas

I received. I would like to request 300 bandanas if I could for my unit. We are getting ready to deploy and my folks love the bandanas. My unit is headquartered in Florence, AL with units spread throughout Northwest, AL. Thank you for your blessings and your ministry." (I thought it was kind of humorous that he said he was shocked at the response.)

"I am a chaplain, currently at the mobilization station at Ft. McCoy, WI. We are taking approximately 1,000 soldiers into Iraq in the coming weeks. I just heard about your ministry from a chaplain that recently returned from Iraq and am SO EXCITED about what you are doing. My troops are young - and many of them are searching. In the next several weeks, I anticipate a greater increase in both individual counseling and chapel attendance. The bandanas that you have would be a great tool to help me encourage troops to turn to God and His Word in the midst of their fear, anxiety, and uncertainty."

"I am a chaplain based in Camp Pendleton and we are gearing up to head out to Afghanistan. Psalm 91 has proven to be an excellent resource to ease the minds and hearts of our Marines as they head into combat. I would like to obtain approximately 1000 of these bandanas for our Marines."

"Thank you and Operation Bandanas for all your hard work and generosity. I have distributed the Psalm 91 bandanas among the soldiers in my unit as well as our many detachments. We have a sick call in our building which brings in many soldiers from other units as well which I also hand them out to. I have underestimated how fast these bandanas have been going out, and I know that you have sent us so many already, but would it be all right to ask for more? If you could, it would be greatly appreciated. Thank you and all of Operation Bandanas for your support and care, it means a lot to us who are currently deployed to Afghanistan to know that people back home are praying for us." T. Wagner, Chaplain's Assistant

"I would love to see if we could get 500 bandanas for our Airmen as they deploy. We have members who deploy almost every month who out-process through our mobility lines, where we give them Bibles and other devotionals on their way downrange. It would be great to also be able to give some of the bandanas to them."

"Could you be kind enough to send me 1000 Psalm 91 bandanas for my Battalion of Marines/Sailors?"

"There are over 575 NMCB 22 Seabees that will be deployed soon. I would like to have a bandana for each of them if possible so that they will have the Psalm while in harm's way to assure them of God's love for them. Getting the word into the hands of those who protect our great nation and our way of life is the best gift that they can receive, for no one knows the time or the hour that they will be called home to eternal life. Your bandanas help make that eternal life a reality where there was none."

"I found one of your bandanas in E. Afghanistan at Tor Kham Gate, with your card. Any way you could send some my way? I'm a chaplain for about 500 west of here.

Thanks for considering this, and may the Lord bless you!"
CH(CPT) Steven Satterfield

"I am a chaplain that has been mobilized to Iraq. Someone brought me a box of the bandanas, which were quickly distributed and gratefully received. Unfortunately, there were nowhere near enough for our battalion, which has about 475 soldiers. The MPs and Bradley crews, in particular, are asking for more bandanas. They like to wear them under their helmets as they go on patrol and provide security for convoys. I have about 200 soldiers who have asked for their own bandanas."

"Our task force is deploying with about 650 soldiers. I would like to have Psalm 91 bandanas available to hand out to them."

"I am currently deployed in Mosul, Iraq. I would like to request 400 bandanas for my Soldiers. Thanks for your work. The bandanas are great!"

"Please send me as many bandanas as you can. This is very much appreciated by our soldiers." Task Force Currahee, Afghanistan

"Our Battalion is in very isolated locations in order to build new FOBs and to provide full spectrum operations to secure the Iraqi population. We would appreciate it if you would please send your bandanas to our 500 Soldiers. Your generosity will aid in our continuing mission."

"First of all I would like to thank you for the bandanas that you donated to the Chaplain we replaced. The troops loved them and they went quick. We are in charge of 2,000 soldiers who go outside the wire and they love the bandanas. Any amount that you can send would be appreciated (especially by our convoy security gunners who ride in the turrets of the gun trucks)." Camp Adder

"I was wondering if my Platoon could get some bandanas. We have 40 Soldiers, but we would take any amount you can give. We definitely need prayers and the bandanas would be reminders for us to pray and thank God for taking care of our unit."

"I could not believe it. I have run out of bandanas and it is hot, hot here! Would you be able to send 250 of those wonderful bandanas to me? It is great to be able to see God's word being spread to our soldiers."

"We will be deploying soon and would like to get 900 of the bandanas."

"Thanks so much for the bandanas. We need them and much appreciate them. If you can send more, please do. The soldiers love them and are begging for more." CH(LTC) Triplett (at the time of this note, Division Chaplain, Third Infantry Division)

"I am a United States Sailor currently deployed to Iraq. I've heard that your organization might support us here, and send us occasional bandanas. Just wondering how to sign up!" FOB Shield, Baghdad

"Many of my Soldiers have come by my office requesting the Psalm 91 bandanas. I found you online. My Soldiers wear the bandanas under their helmets to help absorb some of the sweat while on foot patrols. I have about 800 Soldiers under my care. I would make sure, with how ever many you can provide, that they would be distributed to my men. As you know, Psalm 91 is widely respected by the fighting man and I am glad to know that even if they don't pick up a Bible, they are still looking to God for help in times of need. Blessings to you and all who help in your ministry."

"We are deploying from Camp Pendleton soon and the Chaplain who we will be taking over for has told us that your bandanas are a great help and uplifting for our troops. Could you send us some more of the bandanas? I believe our goals are the same and we would benefit our service members with your help."

"I minister to young men going through Infantryman training so we have up to 1400 soldiers training here when all our companies are in cycle. If I could get 1000 bandanas that would be great; any more than that would be awesome. In this setting that number of 1400 is repeated several times throughout the year as thousands of soldiers are trained and then sent out to join units worldwide. Most of the young men we train will find themselves in combat within weeks of departing Fort Benning so what you do is indeed spiritually strategic for the lives of these young men. Thanks again for all you are doing and may God richly bless you tenfold for all your efforts!" CH(CPT) Tim Cross

CH Cross distributing Psalm 91 bandanas to our troops training for battle.

"My Chaplain was recently at a conference and picked up one of your packaged bandanas with Psalm 91 printed on the front, and I wanted to get in touch with you to see how we can obtain some of these for our training soldiers. Currently our Training Element has trained over 9,000 National Guard Soldiers from all over the country. We are continuing to receive more soldiers for training, and I believe this would be an awesome item to be able to pass to those who would like to have one on their deployment." Camp Roberts, California

"As a new Christian deploying to a hot zone, this promise from God is very comforting. If your organization has any bandanas, I know that my battalion would love to have them for our upcoming deployment. Thanks for everything you do."

"I am in need for more bandanas. Can I possibly get another 500?"

"The reason that I am writing and asking for 1000 bandanas is, that with the help of the Chaplain and a few of the Marines, we have been able to get a go ahead to allow for the wear of the Marine Pattern Psalm 91 bandana under our helmets. This is huge for my Chaplain's ministry and does two very important things. First, of course, is obviously spreading the love that God has for His children through the strong and encouraging words of the Psalm; and second is the fact that during the hot months in Afghanistan these bandanas have the potential to save lives by keeping the sweat out of the eyes. We do have to concern ourselves with getting enough for everyone in the unit and within our chaplain's charge. What can we do to make this happen?"

"Almost all of the American Forces going into and out of the Middle East pass through Kuwait. I was recently contacted by the Theater Support Command Chaplain and he asked me to see if you would be willing to send him some bandanas. He could use a thousand but will take whatever you can send." CH(LTC) Jeffrey D. Houston (at that time, Deputy XVIII ABN Corps Chaplain)

Once sent, I received this email from CH(COL) Lanious:

"Thank you for your generosity and thoughtfulness in providing the Psalm 91 bandanas for the service personnel at the Theater Gateway in Kuwait. Your support helps to boost morale and assures us that we are not forgotten. It is a direct and practical way of supporting the troops."

Even though most all of our requests are for large numbers at a time, occasionally I also receive requests from individual soldiers wanting them for themselves and a few extra for their battle buddies. It is just as meaningful and pulls at the heartstrings:

> "How do I go about requesting these bandanas for me and my deployed co-workers in Iraq? Me and 4 other soldiers from my unit are out here supporting the mission. The rest of our unit is spread out throughout Iraq. Thank you so much for what you guys do!"

> "I'm a soldier currently stationed in Iraq and would love to have one of your bandanas. I would really appreciate it if you could let me know how I can get one, if you need money or whatever. If you have a few extras, I'm sure I can find guys to take them with no problem. I'm in the Texas National Guard out of Irving, Texas. Thank you so much for supporting us. It means more than you can imagine."
> Camp Adder (Tallil)

To all those who helped meet these requests, THANK YOU! You have and are making a difference in the hearts, minds, and souls of our incredible servicemen and women.

CHAPTER 21

Pick Up! Delivery! Mail!

Getting Bandanas to Our Troops in All Ways Possible

Picking up Bandanas.

Delivering Bandanas.
18th Airborne Corps and 82nd Red Falcons

Marine Corps Base Camp Lejeune.

Mailing Bandanas.
I'm a frequent visitor to the Post Office and on a
first name basis with all who work there!

CHAPTER 22

Faith Overcomes Fear

In February, 2005, our youngest son, Andrew, was preparing for his first deployment to Afghanistan. (This was almost two years before I began Operation Bandanas.) He was assigned to the 173rd Airborne Brigade in Vicenza, Italy, and his dad and I had not seen him in quite some time since his unit was based overseas. My husband and I made plans to spend Christmas and New Year's in Italy with Andrew before he deployed. We had so much fun traveling and spending time together. His dad and I did our best not to think about the next month and Andrew's deployment.

It was approaching time for our return home. We knew when we told him good bye it would be a tough one knowing our 25 year old "baby boy" was off to war. Of course, he, like so many of our incredible young men, was excited and anxious to do his duty and get on with it. He was fit, trained, and ready to put his training into action. He was a 1st Lieutenant, and he would be a platoon leader of approximately 40 young men--a big responsibility for our son.

I awoke one night, my husband and son sleeping, and became overwhelmed with the thought of my boy going to Afghanistan. My imagination got the best of me and all kinds of frightening thoughts came to mind. I know I'm not supposed to worry because faith and worry are opposites. I talked about that that in a previous chapter; but I just couldn't seem to help myself. Worry is one of the most powerful weapons that the devil uses against us. And along with worry, comes fear, which is another weapon he uses to paralyze us. His power over me was brief, though, because I knew what I needed to do...I needed to go to God with my worry and fear.

I started praying for Him to look after Andrew, to give him what he needed to lead, to protect him in every way, and to return him home safely to his dad and me. I also asked God to do one of those things that Christians sometimes do in times of crisis...I asked Him to please allow me to randomly open the Bible and speak peace and reassurance to me.

I placed my Bible in my hands and prayed again for God to reveal something to me to remove my fear and worry. Then I opened it. My eyes fell upon Acts 27. Not knowing which verse to zero in on, I decided I would read the whole chapter. I hurriedly and expectantly read through it hoping to find my release from this fear that I was allowing to dominate my mind.

When I finished the chapter, I sat there for a minute, feeling disappointed. I didn't find what I was looking for. The entire chapter was about Paul as a prisoner on board a ship being sent to Rome to be handed over to the Roman authorities. I was very familiar with the passage, but I was confused about what I was supposed to get out of it to reassure me. I thought maybe my random opening of the Bible was just a silly thing to do.

I decided to read the chapter one more time, word by word, more slowly, to see if I had missed something. And there it was in verse 22! I found what I had been hoping for, the answer to my distress and fears! I had totally missed it before, but now it was like a neon sign that lit up the page!

The ship was about to shipwreck and everyone on board was afraid for their life. The storm had gone on for days. Paul spoke to them in verse 22, "Now I urge you to take heart, for there will be no loss of life among you, but only the ship." There it was, jumping right off of the page, "...take heart, there will be *no loss of life*...." The heavy, burdensome weight that I had awoken with was almost immediately lifted. I breathed a huge sigh of relief and thanked God for His faithfulness in my request of reassuring me through His Word.

That's what God's Word will do for you. It will speak to you, and it will comfort you and give you rest and peace. Jesus tells us, "Come to Me all you who labor and are heavy laden, and I will give you rest" (Matthew 11:28). I went to Jesus heavy laden, and He gave me rest. Another verse I thought of (and one of my all time favorites): "You will keep him in perfect peace whose mind is stayed on You, because he trusts in You" (Isaiah 26:3). Notice the verb "will" in both of those passages. God is pretty emphatic that He *will* give you rest and He *will* give you peace. But notice also that we must do something...we must "come" and we must "trust." I was so thankful that I knew Him well enough to boldly and freely come to Him, place my trust in Him, and receive His promises. I went back to bed and rested in perfect peace for the remainder of the night. I recall that I had a smile on my lips as I drifted off.

In the morning, I shared with Andrew and my husband how and what God had spoken to me through His Word. I wanted it to reassure Andrew also that God would be with him and that God would see that he and his troops would all return home safely. I think he found comfort in that too.

Andrew did have some near misses...rollovers, an IED he felt sure had been intended for his platoon, but was detonated by a civilian vehicle just ahead of them, incoming rockets, an area of mines unbeknownst to them that they had stopped in to take a break...and those were just the ones he told us about. But they were *misses*. I'm sure there were other times that God protected them, but perhaps not quite so dramatically and clearly visible to them. He did return home safely; he and his entire platoon!

Daily, my son and his soldiers would suit up with their armor and battle gear, get in their humvees, and set out for patrols, both foot and mounted. If you've ever seen pictures of Afghanistan, you know how desolate, austere, and mountainous it is; yet day after day, we have courageous young men and women who drive out of the safety of their FOB (Forward Operating Base), putting themselves, without hesitation, in harm's way to search for an enemy who is determined to bring destruction and death to them; and to bring it within the borders of America.

From the pictures that Andrew sent to us, my husband and I could see that there were mountains on both sides of them with a narrow, dusty, sometimes muddy, dirt pass between. At other times there were mountains on one side and a big drop on the other. Those pictures reminded me of what I had seen in the old western movies that I watched as a child...the bad guys lying in wait up in the mountains to ambush the good guys on the pass below. It is like that for our troops; there is an enemy, bad guys, waiting to ambush or set off explosives that would maim and kill our good guys. There were times when my son and his platoon wouldn't return to the safety of their FOB for days. But they *would* all return safely. And in those moments while he was deployed when I would awaken in the night--which is a common occurrence if you have a loved one deployed-- I would cling to God's word to me that night in Italy..."there will be no loss of life." And peace and rest would return.

Andrew with soldiers of 2nd PLT, C Company, 1-508th PIR
Afghanistan, 2004

CHAPTER 23

Praise, Protection, and a Prayer
From our oldest son, Rob, Iraq, 2006

"Our Company has been in contact no less than 40 times, had 2 IEDs detonate against us, and had an entire house with an assault force inside blow up seconds after the realization that the structure was booby-trapped and the force evacuated. Our vehicles are peppered with numerous impact marks from small arms rounds and we have had 3 windshields hit center-mass where the driver sits with no penetration or effect on the driver. We have had countless RPGs and hand grenades detonate near us with little or no effect. I ask that you give praise for the protection we have been afforded to date.

My prayer requests are for continued mental sustainment and clarity of thought when conditions are difficult and chaotic; for strong leadership and wisdom for myself and others in leadership positions when actions and decisions have to be made in critical seconds; for protection from the enemy, for his inaccuracy and our steeled accuracy; for both calmness and for aggression when situations require either; for my faith to not be compromised by difficult and ambiguous circumstances.

I especially pray for all of the more than 3000 families who have lost someone here and in Afghanistan. I pray for their comfort and for wise and Christian friends for them to turn to. I pray for my family and my beautiful wife and my 2 incredible boys and my 3rd son on the way. (They now have 4 sons.) These are blessings I am far too undeserving to have been given. But I pray for their sustainment as I have only been home for five months out of the past eighteen. No deployment is easy, and it is not normal for a woman to be separated from her husband for such long periods of time or for children to be without a fatherly influence for long durations.

I pray that our Lord's will be done, and I pray that all of my men and myself are within that will and that we will all return home to our loved ones soon. I am personally tired." (Rob did return home safely time and again. Sadly, some of his friends didn't.)

As a mother praying Psalm 91 over her two sons deployed numerous times to Iraq and Afghanistan, there were several specific verses that I claimed over them:

> "Surely He shall deliver you from the snare of the fowler and from the perilous pestilence" (verse 3). A snare is a trap, and I thought of the traps of IEDs (Improvised Explosive Device), roadside bombs, and ambushes that had been set for my son and all of our servicemen and women. The fowler is the hunter and the hunter in Iraq and Afghanistan is the enemy of our soldiers, the Taliban and Al-Qaeda. The perilous pestilence is for deliverance from any kind of physical illness or plague.

> "You shall not be afraid of the terror by night, nor of the arrow that flies by day, nor of the pestilence that stalks in darkness, nor of the destruction that lays waste at noonday" (verse 5). Rob did night missions into Sadr City, Iraq, just about every night, so the terror by night was very real to him. I prayed courage for my sons.

> "For He shall give His angels charge over you to keep you in all your ways" (verse 11). This is another prayer for their protection --angels to encamp around them and guard them.

I had actually begun praying verse 11 over all three of my sons early on in their careers, before I was ever called to begin this ministry. I would pray it over my soldier sons as they went through difficult training in preparation for combat: Ranger School, Airborne School, Air Assault School, and Special Forces Qualification training; and I prayed it over my middle son while he was serving in Uzbekistan with the Peace Corps. Our young men and women in uniform need to be remembered as they train because training in itself is very dangerous and hazardous to their health and well being. Whether training, deploying, or returning home...they need and deserve our constant, vigilant uplifting.

Rob in Afghanistan, 2005.

CHAPTER 24

But Why?

As I write about my sons returning safely from their deployments, I am very sensitive to and saddened by the fact that there have been thousands of sons and daughters of America who have been killed in Iraq and Afghanistan. Mothers, fathers, wives, children, and family members prayed the same prayers that I did for my sons and yet their precious loved one paid the highest price of freedom with the ultimate sacrifice...their young lives. Our servicemen and women know the risks, but they are willing to take those risks even if it means giving their life in exchange for our freedom and safety. They are our home town, home grown heroes, and they deserve our highest honor and respect.

Psalm 91 is a prayer of protection. And there have been testimonies from many young men and women protected and delivered from harm. God's word is powerful, and when we claim it, we draw comfort, courage, and strength from it; and we receive its promises. But we also know that others who carried or wore the bandana have been taken from us. We will never understand why some are spared and not others, except to try to rationalize it as being either "their time," or "not their time." But that is little comfort when you receive the knock at the door and see a casualty notification team on the other side.

The Bible is filled with the account of the saints who were martyred and died cruel deaths, particularly in the New Testament (read Hebrews 11:35-40). There is evil in the world. And there are enemies of our nation who want to kill, maim, and destroy our men and women defending our nation and others. We live in a fallen, sinful world.

We will never fully comprehend on this side of heaven the how and why of God's sovereignty. "My thoughts are not your thoughts, nor are your ways My ways," says the LORD. "For as the heavens are higher than the earth, so are My ways higher than your ways, and My thoughts than your thoughts" (Isaiah 55:8-9). One thing we do know...as Christ Followers, to be absent from the body is to be present with the Lord, and we can rejoice in that! Our full inheritance is received on that day. We must choose to believe and trust in Him even when we don't understand the difficult circumstances of life.

I can't give you an answer to "why." No human can. But I know that God is filled with compassion. He tells us in Psalm 34:18, "The Lord is close to the brokenhearted and saves those who are crushed in spirit" (NIV). He sees our tears and hears our weeping. And He is filled with love: "For as high as the heavens are above the earth, so great is His love for those who fear Him..."(Psalm 103:11, NIV). I would encourage you to take time to read the entire chapter of Psalm 103. It is a beautiful picture of our Father's love and compassion.

Have you ever given thought that God doesn't view death as we do? According to His words from Psalm 116:15, "Precious in the sight of the Lord is the death of His saints." It is a time to welcome His precious children home. He has a very special place prepared for them. Those of us still on earth are the ones to be pitied. We are still waiting for that great reward! "No eye has seen, no ear has heard, no mind has conceived what God has prepared for those who love him" (I Corinthians 2:9, NIV).

We may have had only a brief time with our loved one here on earth; but for those of us who have received Jesus as Savior and Lord, we will spend eternity together. Life here on earth is temporary and brief. It's a journey, not a destination. Heartache, pain, and sorrow are real and raw. There are days when the anguish and loss is almost unbearable. But one day there will be no more tears and no more pain as we step into eternity and see our loved one(s) again. Our faith has been put to the test, but we keep on trusting in the only One who can carry us through. "Where, O death, is your victory? Where, O death, is your sting?....Thanks be to God! He gives us the victory through our Lord Jesus Christ" (I Corinthians15:55-56, NIV).

I have quoted numerous verses from the Bible in this particular chapter. There is a good reason for that --God has all the answers! He wrote the book! We may still not understand all of it, but Scripture is filled with His promises like those found in Psalm 91. (I had a soldier tell me that he kept a Psalm 91 bandana in each of his boots so he could stand on the promises of God. Isn't that precious?) That's why Operation Bandanas began—to point those searching for meaning and purpose in life to His Word which has all the answers to whatever it is they are searching for.

My desire and passion and the mission of Operation Bandanas has been to give every soldier on the battlefield an opportunity to know the one true God and to receive Him as Lord and Savior. Should they lose their life on the battlefield, or whenever that time comes, they will then receive eternal peace and joy in the presence of Christ. I know it's only one passage of Scripture, but I'm praying that *one* passage will open the gates of heaven to many. I want our soldiers to have a fighting chance at salvation. If a Psalm 91 bandana can lead them to that, then we will have fulfilled our mission!

> *"I have fought the good fight, I have finished the race, I have kept the faith. Now there is in store for me the crown of righteousness which the Lord, the righteous Judge, will award to me on that day—and not only to me, but also to all who have longed for His appearing"* (2 Timothy 4:7-8, NIV).

The next chapter is very poignant and personal, written from the heart of a Gold Star mother, Maria Simpson, who has had to bear the burden of losing a son on the battlefield. For those who may not be familiar with the designation, Gold Star, these are the family members who have lost a loved one in war. Maria's son fought the good fight, finished the race, and kept the faith.

CHAPTER 25

Gold Star Connection
Maria Simpson's Tribute to Her Son, Abe

REMEMBERING ABE
March 16, 1985 - November 9, 2004

My baby, my child, my son,
You first made me a mother, forever so.
To God I gave you back – you were never mine to keep,
Though closest to my heart.
You grew up and away with time, and it was right;
Further from me, closer to Jesus;
Independent before Him.
You let us in on your choices, but you made them
Alone before God – confident before Him.
It was you and God that chose your path,
You and God that accepted and bore
The consequences of those choices – without regret.
A man you were before Him and before us.
He made you so beautiful!

And then your time became complete.
Your days were finished here – continued there.
By the choice of one to do evil – you were sent
Abruptly away from this earth, to return only in glory one day

Beside your King.
And even now you see His face before you,
And you join with angels in worship
Because of our Savior's promise to
All those who put their faith & trust
In Jesus Christ alone for their eternity.
Our hope is true – your hope is now realized.
And here we camp – at the edge of eternity, as we long to see what you see,
And we will...

~

Maria Simpson

"So when this corruptible has put on incorruption, and
this mortal has put on immortality, then shall be brought
to pass the saying that is written: 'Death is swallowed up
in victory'" (I Corinthians 15:55).

Abe loved backpacking and was the most loyal friend you could find. He
was an Eagle Scout and a Christian. He loved San Jose del Cabo where he
served on two mission teams in 2002 to share his faith and to assist a sister
church. He was planning a trip there as soon as he got back.

Abe wanted to be a Marine because if he was going to serve, he wanted
to be part of the best. It was his life goal, and then to become LAPD. He
was very bright, but wanted very much to be known as just one of the regular
guys. He got a perfect score on the ASVAB (Armed Service Vocational
Aptitude Battery).

Two marks of his heart and character that I love are: before he left he
told us and others that if anyone was to die, it would be better that it would
be him, because he was prepared to meet his God, and the others weren't.
He also wanted to be infantry to be able to share his faith with those who
were at the tip of the spear, since they were in the most danger.

He also wrote to a friend that he had chosen not to pursue a romantic
relationship while he was a Marine because he didn't want to mess up
someone's life if anything happened to him. As a result, he never dated,
though he had many friends that he spent all his time with while he was
home.

Abe treasured his friends and family, and he always wanted to do the right thing; this is why he served. One of his comrades who helped inventory his stuff to send home said that the unique thing about Abe was that there was nothing they couldn't send home; nothing the family shouldn't see. He also said that Abe was never "shaken" by the things that got to the rest of them. He found his hope, strength and stability in the word of God.

Abe Simpson, KIA 09 NOV 04, Fallujah, Iraq.
"All gave some. Some gave all."

Maria also sent another tribute to one of our finest:

Jonathan James Simpson
September 28, 1981 - October 14, 2006

Though Jonathan was born and raised in Quebec, he obtained his U.S. citizenship on July 4, 2001, and enlisted in the U.S. Marine Corps the next day. He proudly considered himself an American. He had a very clever sense of humor, devotion to his family and friends, and became a Marine to serve his country and for the opportunity to push himself to the limit physically and mentally.

Jonathan was very bright, and though he was looking for the challenge and esprit de corps that the Marine infantry offered, he was persuaded to become a C-130 Navigator. After completing all his schools, he was stationed in Okinawa for nearly a year, when his cousin, Abraham Simpson, was killed in Iraq. Jonathan flew to California to serve as a pall bearer for his cousin, and gained a new resolve to become the infantryman he had always wanted to be. He went back to Okinawa for one more year, then switched to try out to be a Recon Marine. He completed the course, was assigned to 1st Recon Battalion and was stationed at Camp Pendleton in March, 2006.

He left for Iraq at the end of September, just after his 25th birthday. He was sending humorous and informational emails while they were settling in and being briefed on the situation, etc. Tragically, Jonathan was shot and killed by a sniper bullet on his first mission in Khalidiyah, October 14, 2006.

This family knows the high price that is paid for our freedom. As do so many others. We owe them all a tremendous debt of gratitude and respect. Never forget.

CHAPTER 26

Fallen Heroes

I have had the privilege of visiting two well known cemeteries honoring our fallen heroes of wars past and present: our Nation's own, Arlington National Cemetery in Washington, DC, called our Nation's most hallowed ground and sacred shrine; and the American Cemetery in Normandy, France, which is situated on a cliff overlooking Omaha Beach and the English Channel. Normandy has 9,387 graves of our patriots and 1,557 names on the Wall of the Missing, most of whom lost their lives in the D-Day landings and ensuing operations. Nothing will bring pause like seeing the white crosses, stars of David, and tombstones of military cemeteries.

A few years ago, as my husband, our youngest soldier son, Andrew, and I were driving through the countryside of Italy before he left for his first deployment to Afghanistan, we came upon a sign which directed us to a lesser known cemetery, The American Cemetery and Memorial of Florence. We found 4,402 American patriots laid to rest there and 1,409 names inscribed on the Wall of the Missing. I am thankful we happened upon it. There are actually 24 military cemeteries overseas where nearly 125,000 American war dead have their final resting place.

Entering a military cemetery gives one a sense of reverence and awe. A humble hush comes over you as you feel you are treading on hallowed ground. You are in the midst of fallen heroes and you tread quietly and respectfully.

Inscribed on one of the colonnades at Normandy:

"THIS EMBATTLED SHORE, PORTAL OF FREEDOM, IS FOREVER HALLOWED BY THE IDEALS, THE VALOR AND THE SACRIFICES OF OUR FELLOW COUNTRYMEN."

Two inscriptions from the chapel:

"THESE ENDURED ALL AND GAVE ALL THAT JUSTICE AMONG NATIONS MIGHT PREVAIL AND THAT MANKIND MIGHT ENJOY FREEDOM AND INHERIT PEACE."

"THINK NOT ONLY UPON THEIR PASSING. REMEMBER THE GLORY OF THIER SPIRIT."

I hope you are teaching and reminding your family, particularly children and grandchildren, of these brave men and women who have fought and continue to fight for their freedom. Perhaps you feel like you don't have a real connection with the military; you aren't related to anyone serving or don't even know anyone serving. I'd like to take this opportunity to give you your connection. These are the sons and daughters of America and although they don't know you either, they are willing to take a bullet, lose a limb, or put their life on the altar of freedom for you. That's your connection.

We are all connected as Americans, and so we respect, remember, support, and encourage those who have *volunteered* to defend and protect our way of life. We remember and honor the living and the dead every Memorial Day, every 4th of July and every Veterans Day. And we remember the families who see them off with their love and prayers for a safe return.

Many do return safely, although war takes its toll emotionally if not physically. No one returns from war unscathed or not changed in some way. We can't always see their wounds. Post-Traumatic Stress Disorder (PTSD), and Traumatic Brain Injury (TBI) are increasing in huge numbers as our military continues into its tenth year of war. The explosions from IEDs that our troops experience are rattling their brains, literally. Some don't make it home to enjoy the embrace of family; they have given their lives and given them honorably and voluntarily. Their families join the ranks of other families who were notified of their loved one's valor, courage, and supreme sacrifice. We honor and remember them all.

As I write this book, it is just before the 10th year anniversary of that terrible day for our nation when we were attacked by terrorists, 9/11/2001. Those pictures on the TV screen early that morning are forever embedded in our minds. Our world changed that day. The safety and security of our homeland was assaulted, and we have never been the same since.

Within a month of the attack, America responded. Our courageous, well trained, and determined armed forces, with weapons and armor ready for battle, put their boots on the ground in Afghanistan. Our troops were given the responsibility to search and destroy al-Qaeda and oust the Taliban regime to let it be known that no enemy will come against our nation without a swift and full force response. Less than two years later, March, 2003, we found ourselves fighting two fronts, Afghanistan and Iraq.

The sons and daughters of America, ten years later, are still responding, fighting an enemy determined and hostile toward them, and bent on continuing to bring death and destruction to our people. Afghanistan is no longer some unknown part of the world. Americans have left their boot prints on the plains, valleys, and mountains of Afghanistan and Iraq. Tragically, not only have they left their boot prints, but also the shed blood of many of our courageous patriots.

I am thankful there are brave, adventurous, daring men and women who are willing to serve our nation in such a way, unconcerned about self, putting the security of others above themselves. I cannot fathom the spirit and courage of the American soldier and his/her continued sacrifice and vigilance; or thank them enough (when referring to the American soldier, I am including all branches of our armed forces).

It often seems that Americans have short attention spans, and as the economy tops the headlines we need to remember, not just on September 11, but every single day, that we have hundreds of thousands of our young men and women still at it. They are doing all that they can and giving all that they have to ensure our safety here at home.

"*Perhaps no one prays for Peace as much as Soldiers, for certainly no one pays the price for war more than they. On July 1st, 2007, I was privileged to lead in a Memorial Ceremony for 5 Soldiers from Task Force Falcon who had been killed the week prior by an IED (Improvised Explosive Device).*

Lives were forever changed that day: mothers lost sons, wives lost husbands, children lost fathers, and Soldiers lost friends. As I saluted the memorial stand and then hugged hundreds of Soldiers grieving the loss of their comrades, I was reminded yet again of the incredible sacrifice these Soldiers are willing to make for each and every one of us. And I was reminded again this 4th of July that freedom is never free...politically or spiritually." CH (MAJ) Jeffrey D. Hawkins, 2-82 ABCT, Camp Taji, Iraq

Memorial Service for a Green Beret.
The Psalm 91 bandana has been framed.

CHAPTER 27

Chris

My husband and I are members of Village Baptist Church in Fayetteville, NC. At one of our Wednesday evening prayer services, we met a soldier, CPL Chris Mason. It is rare to have single soldiers attending week night services, but Chris was there just about every Wednesday night. Because of his regular attendance, we became friends, often sitting with him.

Chris told us he had enlisted on his 30th birthday two years prior. Most soldiers enlist at a much younger age, but he said he was ready to serve his country and was hoping, being older and more mature, he could be a good example to the younger troops. He was a good ole patriotic Alabama boy, laid back, friendly, and easy to talk to.

We were moving from one house to another. Since Chris was a big, strong guy, we asked him if he could help us with the move. Without hesitation, he said he would be glad to. After an evening of moving furniture, he stayed for dinner. We sat and talked for quite some time around the table. He was in no hurry to leave. I think he was really enjoying just relaxing and being in a home environment with a mom and dad. I could tell his family meant a lot to him as he talked about them. It was an enjoyable evening.

It was getting close to Chris's deployment to Iraq. I was planning on giving him a big farewell hug before he left. But he slipped out quietly, and I didn't have that opportunity. Maybe that was the way he wanted it.

My husband and I were reading the newspaper one morning when my husband caught a glimpse of a picture of Chris...then the headline..."Corporal is Killed in Iraq Bombing." I went numb in disbelief. I felt like my heart dropped from my chest and went into the pit of my stomach. This was the first soldier that we had actually known personally to be killed. I could still picture him sitting around our table. This good looking, tall, strong young soldier who loved the Lord was killed on November 28, 2006, by a roadside bomb that struck his vehicle near Bayji, Iraq.

The notice in the paper wasn't the typical death notice about a soldier that the military writes up when one of their own dies. It gave the usual information and bio about him...who he was assigned to, 1st Battalion, 505th Parachute Infantry Regiment, 82nd Airborne Division; comments from his Company Commander; being posthumously promoted and awarded the Bronze Star Medal and Purple Heart. But the notice went on to say that while home on leave in October, Chris had been asked to speak at Life Church of Mobile, Alabama. "There's 160,000 American soldiers kicking tail over there! And wherever freedom goes, the gospel's soon to come right after," Chris told the congregation.

Chris's brother, 2nd LT Garland Mason, III, told the *Mobile Press-Register* that his brother was not afraid to die. "He was very passionate about Christ, and because he was so in love with Christ he was able to give his life away for other people." Garland called Chris, "a great brother and a great Christian." He read from an email Chris wrote just hours before his death..."I know that things seem at times to be out of control, but just hold on to the fact that it is God who is in control."

There was another article about Chris in our local newspaper, the *Fayetteville Observer*, two weeks later, picked up from the AP, dated December 14, 2006. The headline was "82nd Airborne Soldier Revered for His Patriotism." There was another picture...but this time it was of his mother, leaving the graveside service for her son, carrying a folded flag held close to her chest, being escorted by Brig. Gen. Joseph Votel, the Assistant Deputy Commander of the 82nd Airborne Division. As a mother of two soldier sons at that time, my heart hurt so badly for her, and I shared in her grief.

The article went on to say that along the route to the cemetery, dozens of people stood roadside with their hands over their hearts, while some held American flags to show their respect. An estimated 400 people gathered at the graveside, where a seven-member honor guard from Ft. Bragg fired three rounds of volleys and a soldier played taps.

The city named a bridge on the city's Bel Air Boulevard for Chris.

Chris's pastor, Dick Braswell, said at his funeral, "We'll see you soon, Chris." I'll look forward to seeing him, too, and giving him that big hug that I wanted to give him before he left for Iraq. A couple of years later, I had the privilege of meeting Chris's brother, Garland, who came to Ft. Bragg as an Army Chaplain. I gave Garland a big hug and upon his deployment, several hundred Psalm 91 bandanas to distribute to his troops.

As I wrote in the "But Why" chapter, we ask and wonder why God would allow this wonderful Christian young man, beloved son and brother, to be taken from his family. It's OK to bear our soul to God and ask "Why?" God is big enough to handle it. Even Jesus, in His humanness, asked "Why?" on the cross. As Christians, we know everything that happens in our lives is for some Higher purpose, even though it often just doesn't make any sense to us.

I feel sure that Chris left a legacy of faith and service to many left behind. I'm sure his mom and dad have many wonderful memories and are proud of the son they had the blessing of raising into manhood. He left them with a message of comfort in his final email..."things seem at times to be out of control, but just hold on to the fact that God is in control." Thank you, Chris. You were one of the best of the best. We'll see you again.

"Greater love has no one than this, that he lay down his life for his friends"
(John 15:13, NIV).

CPL Chris Mason, one of our nation's finest.
KIA November 28, 2006, Iraq

CHAPTER 28

Blue Star Connections

One of the extra blessings (and there have been many) I have received through this ministry is that I have made friends with other moms and dads and wives of servicemen, some of whom I have been blessed with meeting and some whom I have never met personally. We are the Blue Star families who have a loved one serving in uniform. I have found as brothers and sisters in Christ, we share a common heritage and a common concern for our loved ones. Having a son, daughter, or husband deployed is another bond that connects us. Because of being personally able to identify with their feelings, I have prayed with some on the telephone, spoken words of encouragement, given counseling, and sent emails of support. We may never meet on this side of heaven, but we have prayed for and with one another for our loved ones, and we have comforted one another.

These are just a few of the emails, requests, and thanks that I have received from family members:

> "I am contacting you hoping by the grace of God that there is a way I might be able to obtain these special bandanas for my son, Justin, & the rest of his Brigade. Justin is with the 1-506, 4th BCT, 101st Airborne, Ft. Campbell, KY, and they are preparing for their upcoming deployment to Afghanistan.
>
> This will be my son's 2nd deployment to Afghanistan. He's only been state side for 14 months. I feel that these

bandanas would be a "light in the darkness" to so many soldiers. If only my son would have had one the first time. I'd give anything to see all those men with a bandana in hand as they prayed before getting on the bus to deploy. I do hope in some way you could help me figure out a way to make this happen. They will be leaving soon. Many thanks and blessings for all you do!" Jennifer Tolly, Illinois

We did figure out a way. I sent Jen brochures to distribute in her church and in her community, she put together a flyer and a fundraiser, and this mom on a mission received enough donations to supply her son's Battalion with 600 Psalm 91 bandanas!

Jen's son, Justin, covering himself with Psalm 91.

"I want to thank you for the bandanas that you supplied our soldiers with before deployment. My husband is in Afghanistan now as I write this. This is our 5th deployment. I just want to thank you for that special gift. At a time like this we all need something to hold on to just to get us through another day. I thank God for His free gift everyday if we only believe in Him. I know He will truly bless you for your

work. Thank you for loving our soldiers like we all should."
A proud Army Wife, CB, Ft. Campbell, KY

A mom in Maine asked her deployed daughter what she could send to her and her unit:

> "The bandana is her group's #1 request, above snacks, notepaper and envelopes, magazines, and hygiene products!"

> "My husband was recently deployed to Afghanistan and I was wondering how I could have a bandana sent to him. We are currently having a hard time financially. We have three kids, a four year old , a 22 month old, and a 2 month old. My 22 month old little boy was hospitalized for a week only 2 weeks prior to his deployment. So my husband is under a lot of stress and I think a little something like the prayer bandana is something that he would appreciate a whole lot." (OpBan not only sent her husband a bandana, but sent extras to share with his battle buddies.)

> "Michael's entire platoon was covered in a prayer of protection in the final swamp phase of Ranger School! When getting to his first duty post, my son began ministering to the young soldiers and ended up discipling two in his home; one was Harrison, a 19 year old PFC (Private First Class). When another unit's outpost was totally overcome with heavy casualties, Harrison volunteered to go immediately as a replacement.

Last week, an IED exploded and Harrison was miraculously saved and just shaken up. Four others died in the explosion, three were his platoon mates. Harrison is trying to find ways to minister to his platoon. I want to send him the Psalm 91 bandanas to pass out to his hurting platoon mates. These bandanas are perfect! I'll get another box for my son upon his deployment." Penny Noel, Oklahoma

"Thank you from the bottom of my heart for what you are doing for our troops. I would like to ask you if you would please send some bandanas to my son-in-law's troops. He is over a group of 50 plus men. There is also 50 plus men who live in the same tent but there is another leader over them. I am handicapped and have no real income. I am praying that someone will donate enough money so this is possible." (And WE did!)

"My husband is currently in Korea and we are expecting a baby boy December 26! This will be his first Christmas without his family, and he is also struggling with missing out on the pregnancy and birth. Our son will be four months old before his tour is through. I think a bandana and a prayer would help bring home to him this year and help him find the strength to get through these trying times for us. I really believe the spiritual support is just what he needs! Thank you for supporting our troops!"

A mom in Florida, Brenda Aderhold, promoted the ministry with a newspaper article in the *Santa Rosa Gazette*. Excerpts from the article titled, "Bandanas are a Labor of Love":

> "Somewhere in Santa Rosa County, there is someone wiping the sweat off of their neck with a bandana....Thousands of miles away, across the Atlantic Ocean, there is another person with a bandana wiping away the sweat from their face, the sand from their ears, and using the cloth to shade their head from the 120 degree heat. That person is a U.S. Soldier, and the bandana they find so many uses for is given to them from people all across the U.S. from a program called Operation

Bandanas. For many soldiers overseas, receiving this piece of cloth...is a thank you letter from people back home....Psalm 91 is printed on the front of every distributed bandana...

The program, which originally started at Ft. Bragg [Fayetteville], North Carolina, has made its way across the U.S., and even down into Santa Rosa County. Brenda Aderhold, a Santa Rosa resident was made aware of the program after her son, who is in the Army told her about the program when he was being shipped to Iraq. Aderhold's son liked the bandana idea so much that he wanted his mother to spread the word about it. He sent her the flyer he received, and from there, Brenda started asking for donations.

...The non-perishable item can be used to bandage wounds, wipe away the constant layer of sand and dirt on a soldier's face, and most importantly, this particular bandana sends a message from the people back home praying for their safe return.

So far, the response from the Santa Rosa community has been overwhelming."

Brenda's son was a battalion chaplain that OpBan provided 550 bandanas to in 2009 upon deployment to Iraq. In August, 2011, CH Aderhold contacted me again for bandanas for his deploying troops.

"I would like to tell you a short but very meaningful, personal story about Psalm 91. When my son was in Marine boot camp in San Diego California, September 2007, I made a copy of Psalm 91 and mailed it to him in a letter.

I went to North Carolina to see him in February, 2009, before his deployment in March to Iraq. I asked if he still had the Psalm 91 I sent him at boot camp. He went straight to his Bible and showed me how he laminated it with scotch tape while in boot camp because they of course did not have the wonderful things we take for granted like a laminating machine at boot camp. Anyway, I asked if he would put that in his wallet and take it with him; so he did.

Christmas of 2009 he and his family came to Texas. He told me he had something very special to give me for Christmas. With my whole family present, and I come from a large family, he gave me a box to open. It was his Psalm 91 bandana he was given in Iraq and carried with him every day. He said he did not wash it, it had Iraq sand and his sweat and if I wanted to wash it that was o.k. What an amazing Christmas gift!!!!! I do not have the words to tell you how much my gift means to me.

I did not wash it, you being a mother I am sure you understand why, and had it professionally framed, and it is now hanging on my living room wall. May the Lord bless you and Operation Bandanas!!!!!!"

Your sister in Christ,
Terri Whitley, Clifton, Texas

My sister in Christ, indeed; we are a part of the same family, the family of God. And this sister and her husband have become an ongoing donor to Operation Bandanas and have blessed many other sons and daughters with Psalm 91 bandanas. I'm praying that these simple bandanas will be the catalyst that brings more into the family!

A request in March, 2010, from Maria Simpson, the Gold Star mom you met in Chapter 25 (this was our very first correspondence):

"My youngest son, Paul, is deploying to Afghanistan. His chaplain has asked for help in obtaining the bandanas for the battalion, and our church is taking donations to fulfill his request. We have a ministry at our church that sends packages once a month to deployed Marines, so we will be supporting them while they are away.

Back in June of 2004, God gave me this Psalm for my oldest son, Abe, as he deployed to Iraq. It was because of verse 16 that I thought he would be coming home alive; however, as Christians we still suffer the same consequences in this fallen world that we live in as anyone else. Abe suffered a direct hit of a rocket propelled grenade (RPG) on the 2nd day of the battle for Fallujah, so he was killed instantly from the blast and shrapnel. I don't know what exactly takes place in those seconds when we pass from this life into eternity, but verse 7 had also been my prayer, and I wonder if he got to see any of that. It doesn't matter now, and I'll ask him when I see him again, if I'm able to recall it! Once again, thank you, Mary, and God bless you for what you do."

Your friend,
Maria Simpson
USMC mom x 2!

Maria's youngest son, Paul.
This mom rallied her church to see to it that all 1000 soldiers in Paul's battalion of marines and sailors receive Psalm 91 bandanas.

113

CHAPTER 29

Under Orders

A bi-monthly update on serving God and Country in Operation Iraqi Freedom
March, 2007
CH(MAJ) Jeffrey Hawkins, 2nd Brigade Chaplain, 82nd ABN

(This was the first newsletter I received from CH Hawkins.)

82ND ALERTED AS LEAD ELEMENT OF PRESIDENT'S "SURGE"

DRB and DEPORD...It's military jargon for Division Ready Brigade and Deployment Order, and in the 82nd Airborne Division, America's 911, it means our Paratroopers can be called upon any time, to go anywhere, for anything. And that's exactly what happened right before Christmas (2006) as we got the news that my Brigade, the 2nd Brigade Combat Team, would depart for Kuwait and await further orders.

So after a whirlwind load out, a beautiful "Candlelight & Vows" marriage renewal ceremony for our military couples and the hardest part of all, saying good bye to Team Hawkins, I was wheels up to Operation Iraqi Freedom VI.

PRE-BATTLE PREPARATIONS READY CHAPLAINS & SOLDIERS IN KUWAIT

Once in Kuwait, long days and short nights of intense, accelerated planning were punctuated by some beautiful moments, as we readied to move forward into Baghdad as the first element of the President's "Surge" policy. The most touching moment was the Pre-Battle Service of Commissioning that I conducted for our Task Force's Chaplains and Assistants. Within hours of their departure to various points and missions in Iraq, we gathered to ask God's blessing for peace, protection, strength, and wisdom. After smiles, tears, sharing, and caring it was time to say, *"It is well with my soul"* and move out.

MINISTRY AT THE TIP OF THE SPEAR IN BAGHDAD

Baghdad is a very dangerous place -- that also makes it a very spiritual place. My greatest privilege as a chaplain is to help Soldiers answer the question, *"If something were to happen to me, where will I spend eternity?"* Every day here means that a gunner gets up in the turret of a Humvee and rides from the security of the "FOB" into the potential insecurity of the streets; a Soldier dismounts and begins to walk a patrol in a neighborhood that has evil people bent on doing evil things; a leader climbs into a helicopter that may, or may not, get to its location. And I haven't met one of them yet who doesn't reflect on the obvious and who doesn't feel comforted by prayer. My mission is to give them Christ.

Operation Bandanas, through the body of Christ, had the privilege, opportunity and blessing to provide Chaplain Hawkins with enough Psalm 91 bandanas to cover his entire Brigade (3500 to 4000 soldiers); and then some! If you recall earlier in the story, LTC Tom Rogers requested enough for his battalion. They were a part of this brigade. We continued to provide the bandanas to the 2nd BCT (Brigade Combat Team) time and again, sending them directly downrange over the next months. The 2nd BCT and the 4th BCT from Ft. Bragg deployed at about the same time, 4th BCT deploying to Afghanistan. These two brigades were the first of many that we have supported over the past five years.

I think of God's timing in calling me to tHIS ministry...November, 2006...the month before the surge into Iraq. God, as always, has a plan; and He has His perfect timing for putting it into action. I'm so thankful and so very blessed to have been chosen and called as the one to initiate His particular plan at that particular time. I'm thankful that I was tuned in, through an intimate, personal relationship, to hear Him speak to me. It never ceases to amaze me at the incredible awesomeness of God at work!

Are you tuned in? Do you have that intimate, personal relationship with your Heavenly Father? If not, fine tune it and receive it now. Your journey will move you in directions you never expected or anticipated!

Chaplain Hawkins praying with some of his soldiers.

CHAPTER 30

Under Orders Final Edition
March, 2008

This is a powerful testimony of the amazing job our chaplains and our soldiers do. How blessed and fortunate these young, new battalion chaplains were to be under the leadership, guidance, and ministry of CH Jeff Hawkins as their Brigade Chaplain.

A Chaplain's Reflections on "The Surge to Baghdad"

"Shouts of joy and victory resound in the tents of the righteous; The Lord's right hand has done mighty things! The Lord's right hand is lifted high! The Lord's right hand has done mighty things! I will not die but live, and will proclaim what the Lord has done...You are my God, and I will give you thanks; You are my God, and I will exalt You. Give thanks to the Lord; for He is good and His love endures forever" (from Psalm 118, NIV, by the Warrior, David).

As I sit on the flight line prepared to leave 431 days, and nights, of Iraq behind --and all the blessings, challenges, and memories this combat deployment has held, I, like David, am overflowing with thanks to God. I am thankful for His protection. For rockets that have not found their mark where I slept, for mortars that have not exploded where I stood, for bullets that have not hit where I lay, and for IEDs that have not detonated where I've driven. I am simply a chaplain grateful to God for having survived the crucible of battlefield ministry. And with all that is within me, I want to make the most of whatever days He grants in the future by honoring His faithfulness in the past.

It's hard to replay nearly 15 months of memories. Some images are a blur; others seem to stand etched indelibly in time. At its beginning, I see a team of Paratrooper Chaplains, from the 2nd Brigade, 82nd Airborne Division, Task Force Falcon, huddled and praying together in Kuwait, perched on the edge of the unknown, alerted as the first unit of the President's "Surge," launched into Baghdad and beyond to stem the tide of ever-increasing violence, propagated by Al-Qaeda insurgents and complicated by Sunni and Shia extremists. I remember thinking to myself, "What will this team of Chaplains and Chaplain Assistants see? What burdens will they hear? What price may they, themselves, have to pay in order to do their duty to God and Country? Then more than ever, I felt both pride and apprehension. Pride in the bravery and fortitude of men who could have been somewhere else, doing something else, with someone else, but instead chose to say "yes" to God's Call to be missionaries in uniform and carry God's presence and grace to those headed into combat. Apprehension in that each and every one of them had families and futures that would have to be put on hold and that would have to hang in the balance as we waited to see what a Country's War and God's Will would bring. I was proud of them, and I was apprehensive for them.

Then thrust into the fray with the charge to *"get off the FOB* (Forward Operating Base) *and into the streets,"* our Falcons set about trying to turn the battle of Baghdad and rescue a country caught in a seemingly downward spiral of bombs, blood, and hopelessness. Though we knew that effort could cost us dearly, I don't think any of us were prepared to be reminded of that cold, hard, fact on the first day, first convoy, first mission outside the wire as the first IED stole the life of our first soldier. Any thought of being able to execute the mission without cost was dashed, and there was a collective sense and sigh of, *"it begins."* And with this came the questions I and our Unit Ministry Teams would hear over, and over, and over again, as the months, and the toll in young lives given to the Cause, mounted: *"Why?"* *"How could God let this happen?"* *"Why Him?"* *"Why her?"* *"Why now?"* *"Why not me?"* Of all the honors and privileges for a chaplain, perhaps none is so burdensome and so blessed as conducting Memorial Ceremonies for our Soldiers. Task Force Falcon invested over 50 of its own for the freedom, peace, and prosperity of Iraq. It remains an infinitely high price, each counted in personal ways by personal friends. Our commitment, in only a way a Soldier can know, is simply to have our lives honor their death. Thankfully, we leave Baghdad infinitely better and safer than when we arrived this deployment--the opportunity of the Iraqi people for peace and freedom is truly before them, having been purchased at dear cost.

Trauma can be a teacher of great lessons. And it is in war that we attend school. I watched young Soldiers become veterans in a matter of months. I watched first term chaplains become subject matter experts inside of weeks as the Spring and Summer of 2007 provided virtually as many combat moments as there were days. I wept with Soldiers who only hours earlier had watched their closest friends burn in Bradleys and had the honor of going with them later that night as they conquered their greatest enemy--fear--and climbed back in their armored chariots to do what must always be done...continue the fight. I remember sitting and listening to the story told again and again, as if caught in an emotional loop, by one medic who saved the life, but could not save the legs, of one of our Troopers at Combat Outpost Callahan as their fortress was barraged by relentless rockets. I remember praying last rites over a Soldier, who looked more the age of my son, as the doctor, exhausted with chest compressions, was pulled off the broken body, his medical team saying, "He's gone, sir...he's gone." I've pulled Iraqi bodies from the street, murdered savagely by their own, and I've pushed American bodies into MEDEVAC helicopters saved valiantly by their own. I've had the painful duty of collecting physical pieces of the enemy's bodies and praying for them, and I've had the powerful duty of collecting emotional pieces of our Soldiers' bodies and praying for them. From urban streets to village fields, from bombed buildings to hospital bed sides, trauma and ministry have gone hand-in-hand for me and our team of Chaplains and Assistants. And this part of the deployment is not something we will ever get over -- it is, however, something we will get through.

I'm not sure all my lessons learned from this rotation of Operation Iraqi Freedom have yet been mentally, emotionally, and spiritually logged, but I am aware of several insights. The first is that God is sufficient. The phrase,

"It's when you discover that He is all you have, that you find Him to be all you need." has more meaning now than ever before in my life.

The second reflection is how proud I am of our young American Paratroopers, who when asked to do incredibly hard things, for indefinite periods of time, in austere and dangerous places, daily rose to the task and challenge courageously. Their ability to look fear in the face and do their duty on too many days to count was simply awe inspiring. I wish every American could have seen what I had the privilege of witnessing daily.

The third insight is the tremendous generosity and outpouring of support from the American people. I was simply amazed by the gracious encouragement from people I never have met, and likely never will meet, through their cards, letters, packages, and gifts. It was beautiful, and it made a wonderful difference for all of us over here so very far from home.

Lastly, I'm humbled at the sacrifice of our Unit Ministry Teams, particularly our Chaplains. All of them are men who have chosen to leave the comfort and safety of their ministries and families at home to assume hardship and danger for the sake of young Americans of every shape and size dressed in camouflage. My chaplains are here because they want to be, not because they have to be. It would be easier to minister elsewhere, but elsewhere is not where they have been called to be. They have been called to be with Soldiers, and that is where they have been...every hour, of every day, and in every way. And for that, and so much more over these past nearly 15 months in combat, I rejoice, as David did,

"You are my God, and I will give You thanks. You are my God, and I will exalt You. Give thanks to the Lord, for He is good; His love endures forever" (Psalm 118:28-29, NIV).

Chaplain Hawkins and I have kept in touch through the years and it has truly been an inspiration, honor, and privilege to support him and his chaplains through the ministry of Operation Bandanas and with our prayers. He gave a powerful message to Village Christian Academy students in Fayetteville, NC, during one of their Chapel services. You can see and hear that message on our DVD and the story he shared that day of a young soldier named Ross, one of our incredible heroes, (who wasn't much older than the Seniors in high school in that Chapel service) and his extreme valor and sacrifice.

This is two of the emails I received from CH Hawkins while deployed:

> "What a HUGE blessing to receive the Psalm 91 bandanas. They are being offered at our convoy prayers and at chapel services and are always well received. Thanks so much for your generosity and faithfulness! Rest assured that they have found their way all across Baghdad in our units with some of the most intense duty. A wonderful ministry!"

> "One 'tradition' you may or may not be aware of that's developed on the part of some Soldiers is having their fellow Soldiers/friends sign theses bandanas as a keepsake before headed home to remind them of God's protection and those who shared it with them."

Another wonderful blessing of leading tHIS mission has been meeting and corresponding with chaplains and soldiers, sailors, airmen and marines; and learning about their remarkable service to our nation and the world.

CHAPTER 31

From the Front

"A few weeks ago I handed out several bundles of your bandanas to Chaplains and their assistants who go out to the forward operating bases. There they work with the soldiers and sailors who are doing the real work. As engineering battalions these guys are pushing tons of dirt, clearing roads, and building just about everything you can imagine could be built in an expeditionary manner. I was out at one of the bases and got stuck in one of their dust storms, the dust so heavy and hanging in the air it looked just like a heavy fog. Apart from the insurgents, one of our greatest issues is the dust. Despite the fact that visibility was about down to a city block, the crews were still out there working. This was before I put in my request for bandanas.

Since we have received them I have used one myself as I walk out to some of the outlying areas of the camp where some of our people work. The dust on the road is like talcum powder 3-4" deep, but as the trucks and MRAPs drove by kicking up the dust, I was well sheltered with my goggles and bandana. The bandanas help keep the dust out of our Sailors, Soldiers, and Marines lungs and keep God's word literally on their mouths. When I am not wearing mine, I have it stuck into the springs on the rack above mine so I can fall asleep and wake up to the Psalm each day.

I just received a call today from one of my Sergeants who asked if I had any more bandanas. Apparently he found a slew of soldiers who wanted one. He told me he could easily distribute a couple hundred, so I told him I would see what I could do.

People generally like it when the Chaplain comes around for a visit, but when the Chaplain offers something that is spiritual *and* practical, it is really a double blessing. Thank you very much." RPCS (FMF) WC

"I'm currently stationed in Iraq to help provide security for logistical convoys throughout the country. My Chaplain here handed out these bandanas to those who wanted one. I think it is a great idea and I really appreciate the generosity of the people who gave to the cause. I carry my bandana with me when I go on missions, so it is always in my pocket where I can pull it out to read the Psalm and draw on God's protection. Thank you for making a difference for the Soldiers here. The more times we read Psalm 91, the more we realize that if we just give our fears and worries to God, He will protect us from harm." 1LT Michael Fellers, Tallil, Iraq

"We are presently serving God and Country in Kandahar City, Afghanistan. Once word got out that we had Psalm 91 bandanas, we ran out immediately. Soldiers wear them under their helmets to keep sweat out of their eyes while on mission, and always ask specifically for the Psalm bandana. Please let me know how we could go about getting more...we would be forever grateful. Your generosity and willingness to support your soldiers overseas has not gone unnoticed or unappreciated.'"

"I wanted to write and give you some feedback on your Operation Bandanas. I'm not sure how often you hear from soldiers overseas that have received your bandanas, but I felt it was important you know the impact they have on the troops. I recently made it in country and was handed one and couldn't wait to sit down to write my thanks. Soldiers all have little items we keep with us when conducting operations. I have a small American flag, a small toy my kids gave me and now my Psalm 91 bandana. I appreciate the service you all are doing and it's churches and citizens such as you that lift our spirits and help us remember how much people do care about us. Sometimes this is a thankless job but you certainly lifted my spirits and my family's now that they know I have this. May God bless you all in everything you do." 1LT S L, FOB Salerno, Afghanistan

"I wanted to take this opportunity before I redeploy back to the States to drop you a personal note of thanks for your kindness and support provided to the Silver Lions as we combated terrorism in Southern Iraq. It is a tough business to spend so long a time away from loved ones and the comforts of home, but the gifts, support and kindness of great Americans like yourself make it that much easier. The bandanas you donated were a terrific morale boost and were genuinely appreciated. Thanks for all you do selflessly to support our soldiers." LTC Scott Taylor

I think it is always amazing how much our troops thank *us* for all that *we* do for them! If you have ever tried to thank a soldier for their service, you'll always hear him/her come back, "Thank *you* for your support." You just can't "out thank" them. What great men and women!

One of our beloved female soldiers!

CHAPTER 32

The Real World

In the summer of 2009, I spent a week in Milwaukee, Wisconsin, for the wedding of my youngest son, Andrew, and his beautiful bride, Stephanie. Andrew had completed his military commitment and was now a veteran of two deployments (27 months) to Afghanistan. My mind was fully focused on the joy of the moment, enjoying the reunion of family and friends and all the excitement that goes with the activities and festivities of a wedding. There were no thoughts of troubles in the world for that week...no thoughts on health care, the economy and the war, no housework, no job...just pure, unadulterated joy! (Something you may find interesting...Andrew and Stephanie are survivors of flight 1549 that went into the Hudson River on January 15, 2009. That was another extraordinary milepost on my journey!)

On the way back home, we flew through Atlanta. It didn't take long for me to move back into the real world. Walking through the terminal, there were soldiers in uniform everywhere I looked; and my heart began to sensitize again to the tremendous sacrifices being made so that I could fly safely to my son's wedding and enjoy the religious freedom of a ceremony honoring to God. It is these sons and daughters of America who have been giving their all since the American Revolution. Those now serving in uniform continue the tradition of selflessly serving our nation, defending it against enemies, both foreign and domestic.

Our men and women in uniform need spiritual encouragement and support more than ever. They are weary of multiple deployments. Many are recovering in burn centers and rehabilitation hospitals, learning to adapt to life with an artificial limb(s). Thousands have been wounded physically and emotionally. Military families all across America are grieving the loss of their loved ones who were willing to pay the ultimate cost of freedom. Homes of our heroes are dealing with the struggles of separation and the adverse impact on their family relationships. These are difficult times for our military. But they do what they do so that we can enjoy and continue "business as usual" in America.

Keeping them in our thoughts and prayers must be a priority. By supplying them with tangible evidence of our prayer support and appreciation, we give them something they can hold on to that reminds them that God is with them at all times. Coming from the generosity of grateful Americans, our little gift of a simple bandana printed with God's words of strength, courage, comfort, and protection could well be just what is needed tucked in the pockets, body armor, and helmets of our troops on the battlefield today... spiritual armor for inspiration and encouragement.

"In battle and in the face of danger and death, he discloses those divine attributes which his Maker gave when He created man in His own image. No physical courage and no brute instinct can take the place of the Divine help which alone can sustain him." General Douglas MacArthur

CHAPTER 33

Grim Headline

"Soldiers' Deaths Expected to Rise" was the headline on the front page of the *Fayetteville Observer* newspaper on July 9, 2010. Excerpts from the first paragraph read, "U.S. troop deaths in Afghanistan, which reached record highs in the past two months, will continue climbing, a top U.S. military commander warned, because the military is trying to oust the Taliban from places where they have never been challenged before." Reading that gave me such a feeling of urgency for putting God's Word into the hands of our troops in any way that we could. The Psalm 91 bandanas we have sent and continue to send downrange is one simple way.

Since I live in a large military community, soldiers and their families are all around us-- in our neighborhoods, restaurants, stores, shops, schools, churches, etc. We also have Marine Corps Base Camp Lejeune just up the road from us. There is a constant rotation of deployments. Families left behind are doing the best they can to "make do," while children are missing their fathers and mothers. This is routine, real life here and at other military installations all across America and around the world. We are grateful and proud of our patriots' valor and their call to serve, but it is difficult and often painful.

It disturbs me to open the front page of our local newspaper and see pictures of Ft. Bragg Soldiers or Camp Lejeune Marines who voluntarily surrendered their lives on the altar of freedom. War and the heartbreaking consequences of war are in our face every day. A 20 year old soldier had been in Afghanistan one week when he was killed; another had just a couple of weeks left before he was due to come home. Still another had had two deployments to Iraq and two deployments to Afghanistan before losing his life on his third tour in Afghanistan. Seven soldiers' pictures headlined the paper one morning, killed within a week in two separate attacks. A Special Forces soldier was killed on his tenth deployment...*tenth*!!!

We will never know the impact our ministry has made. But I like to imagine that one day in heaven someone may come up to me and others who ministered through Operation Bandanas and thank us for the bandana that we sent to him/her; and perhaps hear them say the Psalm 91 bandana they received was the beginning of their journey of faith that led them to a relationship with Jesus. After all, at the end of our journey on earth, all that will matter is what we did with Christ. Our days are numbered, and we only have a short time to make the decision that will determine where we will spend eternity. If you died today, do you know for sure where you would spend eternity?

I know you join me in praying: God, be near to everyone of those serving in harm's way, draw them to You, and bring them safely back home to their families. Provide for their every need. Keep them emotionally stable, physically fit, and protected from evil, sickness, and injury. Deliver them from the snare of the fowler and the perilous pestilence; cover them with your feathers and give them refuge under Your wings; be their shield; give your angels charge over them to guard them in all their ways; be with them in trouble; and show them Your salvation. And give wisdom to those in leadership positions making decisions that will determine the course of our history.

CHAPTER 34

A Week in the Life of a Chaplain Downrange
From Chaplain Rod Gilliam
FOB Farah, Afghanistan
July, 2011

My assistant and I make up what is known as a Unit Ministry Team (UMT). Our goal is to "Bring God to Soldiers and Soldiers to God." It is a sacred honor to do what we are called to do. One in which my assistant and I are deeply committed. We accomplish this by:

* Nurturing the Living
* Caring for the Dying
* Honoring the Dead

A typical week for my assistant and me is to travel in a convoy during the first half of the week to several of our outposts where our Soldiers are staying. Typically we offer a field worship service, my assistant is a skilled guitarist and worship leader, and I offer the preaching of the Word. We always end our service with Holy Communion. It's really kind of a neat sight to see a field service, with so many of our Soldiers attending in some obscure outside location in a battle zone. There really are very few atheists in combat.

After we provide a worship service I usually circulate to all the guard checkpoints, med station, command center, mechanics work area, cooks, etc, to see how they are all doing. Usually I have a string of Soldiers dealing with personal issues either from the home front or the battle front. I'll take the time to counsel and pray for each one. There are a lot of similarities as to what I do with Soldiers and our behavioral/mental health professionals do when they come on site. I guess the biggest difference is that, as a chaplain, I bring a spiritual dimension into the counseling arena. When we are done at one outpost, we hitch a ride with a convoy and go to another to do it all over again.

By the latter part of the week, (around Thursday) we make our way back to our Forward Operating Base (FOB). There we do much of the same; circulate with Soldiers, counsel, provide worship opportunities. It is all very fulfilling. Occasionally, both on the FOB and at one of our outposts, I will get called to a Medical Station to meet with the wounded. There, while the doctors are working with the patient, I will be next to his side talking/offering words of comfort and praying with him. This is one of the harder things about the job.

I was with a Soldier of ours who died at the beginning of our deployment and another critically wounded in a firefight with the Taliban. As the unit Chaplain, I was busy conducting a memorial service, providing "Traumatic Event Management" counseling as well as one on one counseling for those closely affected, along with the basic chaplain duties of bringing Soldiers to God and God to Soldiers. In a general sense, it's a true honor to know that I can see a Soldier's loved ones some day to tell them I was there in their loved ones final moments, and that I know beyond a shadow of a doubt that this Soldier was ready to meet his Maker.

This serves to remind all of us that what we are doing is very real. As a chaplain, I cannot emphasize how important it is for each of us to have made our peace with God. What encourages me as I minister is that many in this environment have "ears to listen." For that I am grateful. You now see why I value your prayers.

For those that are Believers, please pray that God keep His divine hand of safety upon us, and that He would offer each of these men and women a perfect sense of peace that only comes from the Prince of Peace, that He would give us the patience of Job, the wisdom of Solomon and the courage of King David. Most importantly, pray that each Soldier may possess the deep, heartfelt assurance that there is an eternal God who loves them without question, who is always near and only a prayer away.

Some of the big projects I am working on:

Pancake ministry - I like to take a George Foreman grill with me to the outposts and serve the troops pancakes. Words can never describe how much they love this. Thanks to those that supply us with the pancake mixes and syrup!

Coffee - need I say more! The chapel is a very popular spot to come each day because I am always brewing a pot of it. Thanks to those who supply us with coffee!

Music Ministry - Someone donated some guitars and strings to our chapel. Soldiers love playing them. There are some very talented individuals out there that only need an instrument in their hand and they'll play it. My chapel is packed to capacity on Sundays. I cannot claim that it is because of my great preaching...by all appearances, people really like coming and listening to good music. I have been blessed this go round to have a great chaplain assistant with incredible musical talents. We take instruments outside the wire and play and sing for the troops.

We are planning on building an outside stage in the back of our chapel and a barbeque pit. We want to organize a weekly event where folks can sit at a picnic table, drink coffee or sodas, relax and listen to live music. The concept is to give the Soldiers a place to perform, play or sing for the troops or just come hang out with their friends and enjoy some live music. I did something similar to this in Iraq and people came out of the woodwork to attend!

132

Library - In the front entrance of my chapel (the foyer area), I am building a library and coffee shop area (think Starbucks with a Christian theme). I want to give the Soldiers on the FOB a nice place to come during the day, relax a bit, read, sit, meditate, pray, whatever; basically a place to unwind. Book donations would be great, inspirational, devotional, historical, psychological, quality literature like what is found in both the classics and semi classics. Soldiers love magazines too - auto, outdoor, news magazines, guns and ammo, hunting, sports, political. Magazines are very popular with the guys on the outposts...they readily consume them. There have many organizations that have been incredibly supportive in this area.

Another item well received is sheets, blankets and pillows. We could use more pillows, and we still have a large need for blankets.

One neat story...the other day a young female Soldier was in my chapel during the week quietly praying. I was at the back of the chapel quietly unpacking care packages. When she finished and arose, she headed to the exit. I asked her if she had received any sheets yet. I had just unpacked some in a care package. She smiled real big and said, "No Chaplain, I haven't. I have been asking God to help me through this place somehow. It seems so dirty here, with very little comforts. Your offer just lifted my day and answered my prayer."

Today is Sunday, so tomorrow I am headed outside the wire to do it all again. Thank you for all your prayers and support. God bless you for your generosity to American Soldiers serving down range.

The email below from CH Gilliam, upon his latest deployment that he writes about above, shows the opportunity of continuing to be able to serve our chaplains as they move to different units:

"While I was a unit chaplain in both the 82nd ABN and the SWTG(A) (Special Warfare Training Group) chaplain at the Special Forces schoolhouse, your ministry was a wonderful means of support to my Soldiers. The bandanas were always very well received. We are due to deploy to Afghanistan (STB, 2BCT, 4ID, Ft. Carson). I have about 500 Soldiers in my organic unit and another 2 x companies of Infantry will be attached with us downrange. Could your ministry please send me some more bandanas so I may hand them out to our Soldiers as we prepare to deploy? I have a total responsibility of just under 700. We would appreciate any amount your ministry would choose to give us." (We "chose" to fulfill his complete request for 700.)

CH Gilliam also shared with us in the chapter, Miraculous Deliverances.

CHAPTER 35

Not Home for Christmas

When Andrew was in Afghanistan during Christmas, 2007, I told him I would send him a Christmas tree and decorations. I thought he would be excited, but he told me it would just make it harder for him as it would be a reminder of just how far from "home for Christmas" he really was. But, with a little coaxing and his blessing, I sent the artificial tree hoping to spread a little cheer in that cheerless, hostile environment. I also sent him some cinnamon scented pine cones and some candles that smelled like cedar, a string of lights, a stocking, a Santa hat and other little sights, sounds, and smells of Christmas. His girlfriend, Stephanie (Andrew's future wife!) sent him the ornaments for the tree. The tree ended up being on the front of their battalion newsletter that was sent to the families of those serving with Andrew. He told me soldiers would visit his office just to breathe in the scents of cinnamon and cedar.

I understood what he was saying, though, about being reminded of not being home for Christmas. I reflected on another Christmas in 1970 when my husband was in Vietnam. That was the year that Karen Carpenter came out with the song, *Merry Christmas, Darling*. She would also sing Bing Crosby's, *I'll be Home for Christmas*. Great songs, but tough to listen to when you are separated from the one you love. When we are away from our loved ones during this season, we miss them more than ever. And when you are wearing a uniform serving in a combat zone, with no family around, it's really tough.

As I sleep in peace tonight and every night, I will give thanks to a Savior, Jesus Christ, born into this world to give me everlasting peace; and I will give thanks for all those serving in uniform keeping watch for me, my home, my family, and my country, so that I (we) can sleep in peace. The following poem expresses "their watch" beautifully:

A SOLDIER'S CHRISTMAS
by Michael Marks

The embers glowed softly, and in their dim light,
I gazed round the room and I cherished the sight.
My wife was asleep, her head on my chest,
my daughter beside me, angelic in rest.

Outside the snow fell, a blanket of white,
Transforming the yard to a winter delight.
The sparkling lights in the tree, I believe,
Completed the magic that was Christmas Eve.

My eyelids were heavy, my breathing was deep,
Secure and surrounded by love I would sleep
in perfect contentment, or so it would seem.
So I slumbered, perhaps I started to dream.

The sound wasn't loud, and it wasn't too near,
But I opened my eye when it tickled my ear.
Perhaps just a cough, I didn't quite know,
Then the sure sound of footsteps outside in the snow.

My soul gave a tremble, I struggled to hear,
and I crept to the door just to see who was near.
Standing out in the cold and the dark of the night,
A lone figure stood, his face weary and tight.

A soldier, I puzzled, some twenty years old
Perhaps a Marine, huddled here in the cold.
Alone in the dark, he looked up and smiled,
Standing watch over me, and my wife and my child.

"What are you doing?" I asked without fear.
"Come in this moment, it's freezing out here!
Put down your pack, brush the snow from your sleeve,
You should be at home on a cold Christmas Eve!"

For barely a moment I saw his eyes shift,
away from the cold and the snow blown in drifts,
to the window that danced with a warm fire's light
then he sighed and he said "It's really all right,
I'm out here by choice. I'm here every night."

"It's my duty to stand at the front of the line,
that separates you from the darkest of times.
No one had to ask or beg or implore me,
I'm proud to stand here like my father before me."

"My Gramps died at 'Pearl on a day in December,"
then he sighed, "That's a Christmas 'Gram always remembers.
My dad stood his watch in the jungles of 'Nam
And now it is my turn and so, here I am."

"I've not seen my own son in more than a while,
But my wife sends me pictures, he's sure got her smile."
Then he bent and he carefully pulled from his bag,
The red white and blue… an American flag.

"I can live through the cold and the being alone,
Away from my family, my house and my home,
I can stand at my post through the rain and the sleet,
I can sleep in a foxhole with little to eat.

137

I can carry the weight of killing another
or lay down my life with my sisters and brothers
who stand at the front against any and all,
to insure for all time that this flag will not fall."

"So go back inside," he said, "harbor no fright.
Your family is waiting and I'll be all right."
"But isn't there something I can do, at the least,
Give you money," I asked, "or prepare you a feast?
It seems all too little for all that you've done,
For being away from your wife and your son."

Then his eye welled a tear that held no regret,
"Just tell us you love us, and never forget
To fight for our rights back at home while we're gone.
To stand your own watch, no matter how long.

For when we come home, either standing or dead,
to know you remember we fought and we bled
is payment enough, and with that we will trust.
That we mattered to you as you mattered to us."

This poem, *A Soldier's Christmas*, became an internet sensation and has appeared in newspapers, magazines and newsletters around the world as well as literally thousands of web sites. When I contacted Michael about using his poem for this book, I found him serving our nation in Afghanistan. He knows personally what he writes about! You can read more of his moving military poetry on his website, www.michaelmarks.com.

Andrew, first deployment, 2004, ready to roll.

CHAPTER 36

From the Front

"Many Soldiers carry the bandanas with them on a daily basis. My prayer, as I'm sure yours is too, is that those that know the true meaning of God's word would constantly be reminded of Him when they see them; and perhaps those who have not surrendered their hearts to the Lord would be gently nudged by His Spirit one day while looking at the words of Scripture on the bandanas. Either way, each of us does a small part planting seeds, and God does the rest. Thank you for being a co-laborer for Jesus Christ and supporting our troops." CH Davis, USASOC

"Thank you! You have made it possible for us to provide a Psalm 91 bandana to every Soldier from our unit, the 18th Fires Brigade (Airborne) who deploys in support of the War on Terrorism." CH Fred MacLean

"On behalf of the soldiers of the 504th Military Police Battalion, I want to extend by heartfelt thanks for your gift of Psalm 91 bandanas this year. These items were extremely popular among our soldiers, and enabled us to meet a physical need, but also opened the door to meeting spiritual needs. You have helped us to have great conversations that have ranged from "checking in" to sitting down and working through some of life's greatest challenges. The result of your generosity has been that soldiers have left our offices or conversations with their material needs met, but also their emotional and spiritual needs met as well. You may never meet the people you have served this year, but rest assured, you have changed lives for the better." For God and Country, CH(CPT) Robert W. Sterling, Battalion Chaplain

"I cannot tell you how many Marines I know who have been blessed through your ministry. Psalm 91 was my mother's favorite Psalm, so I was greatly encouraged myself seeing the bandana for the first time. Thank you for the donation of bandanas for my upcoming outreach. I know my Marines will truly appreciate this." Very respectfully, LT Jeremy Blythe, CHC USN

"It is very encouraging and "God sent" seeing the faithfulness and loving heart you have for us. It actually gives Soldiers strength and encouragement. With the sacrifice of time, giving and through your diligent prayers, we feel our sacrifice is worth it all. I have traveled to Leatherneck and Shindand visiting and ministering to Soldiers and Unit Ministry Teams we support. As we strive for victory over those who attacked our homeland, our Servicemen fight alongside our NATO friends to prevent the insurgents from taking land, homes, families, peace and freedom from the people of Afghanistan. In war, warriors go through various stages of emotions from high energy excitement to feelings of depression. As you are well aware, war takes a toll on servicemen and women, families and those who live in this country. We look forward each day seeing packages and letters come in for the troops. Thank you!!! May God provide and bless you with more than you can give." CH(MAJ) Michael Frailey and SSG Trevor Rush

"Thank you for your passion for the Lord and vision to get the word of God into the possession and hearts of soldiers. In the face of a broken world filled with chaos, death, separation from loved ones and the uncertainty of war, God's word comes as an unmovable foundation and is a rock of refuge. As Jesus said in Mark 13:31, 'Heaven and earth will pass away, but my words will never pass away.' The stability of Christ and His word is what soldiers need on the battlefield today. Some of these soldiers would never open a Bible or the door of a chapel, but they will reflect on the words of Psalm 91 during the dark hours of the night watches. These words can be the catalyst that draws them closer to the Lover of their souls and ultimately to salvation. It is an honor to serve alongside you in Christ's body. May the Lord continue to bless you and your ministry." By His Grace, For His Glory, J.R. Lorenzen, 18th Fires BDE Chaplain

Delivering bandanas to CH(CPT) Lorenzen in PX parking lot.

Under His Wings
by Peggy Joyce Ruth

"He shall cover you with His feathers, and under His wings you shall take refuge..." (Psalm 91:4).

My sister in Christ, Peggy Joyce Ruth, (whom I have never met yet!) has written a book, *Psalm 91, God's Shield of Protection*. She has printed several different editions, but the one that I first received and became familiar with was her Military Edition. She has sent thousands upon thousands of these books as gifts to chaplains and our armed forces serving in all parts of the world and through organizations that support our military. I was thankful to be contacted by her shortly after I began Operation Bandanas, and we have become partners in sharing the promises of Psalm 91. I even had the privilege of writing something that was included in one of her recent editions. Her books take the Psalm, verse by verse, and beautifully interprets each verse. One of my favorite illustrations that she shared was from verse 4a..."He shall cover you with His feathers, and under His wings you shall take refuge..." Here is her interpretation:

> "My husband, Jack, and I live out in the country, and one Spring our old mother hen hatched a brood of baby chickens. One afternoon, when they were scattered all over the yard, I suddenly saw the shadow of a hawk overhead.

I then noticed something that taught me a lesson I will never forget. That mother hen did not run to those little chicks and jump on top of them to try to cover them with her wings. No!

Instead, she squatted down, spread out her wings and began to cluck. And those little chickens, from every direction, came running to her to get under those outstretched wings. Then the hen pulled her wings down tight, tucking every little chick safely under her. To get to those babies, the hawk would have to go through the mother.

When I think of those baby chicks running to their mother, I realize it is under His wings that we may take refuge...but *we have to run to Him.*

God does not run here and there, trying to cover us. He said, "I have made protection possible. You run to Me!" God is deeply committed to us --yet at the same time, we can reject His outstretched arms if we so choose. But when we do run to Him, in faith, the enemy then has to go through God to get to us.

What a comforting thought!"

I love how Peggy Joyce has illustrated God's protection and love for us. Isn't that a beautiful picture of our Heavenly Father? I can just picture Him with His outstretched arms waiting to welcome us into His embrace and literally covering us with His love and protection. I can find refuge in Him, and He will protect me from my enemy. All I have to do is run to Him! Peggy Joyce's website is www.peggyjoyceruth.org.

CHAPTER 38

Phone Call

Most of the correspondence I have with chaplains and the troops is via email, but occasionally I'll get a personal handwritten note which is always very special. I once received a phone call from a soldier in Afghanistan who called to tell me thank you and how much the bandana meant to him. I wasn't home at the time, so he left a message. I was just sick that I didn't get to talk to him, but I kept that message for a long, long time on my phone.

I was quite pleasantly surprised one morning when I actually received a phone call from a Marine at Marine Corps Base (MCB) Camp Lejeune. Thank goodness I was home to talk to him! He told me he carried his Psalm 91 bandana with him at all times and would read and claim it every morning. He credited God's words of protection with saving his life when he and four of his battle buddies were hit by a mortar. All survived the hit and all had a bandana. He also told me he was just now able to talk about it.

This Marine said he still had a long road to recovery. He received shrapnel over the entire left side of his body, has titanium steel in his jaw, 30 pieces of shrapnel in his left knee, serious injury to his left foot and hand, has TBI (Traumatic Brain Injury) and PTDS, but was still thankful he was able to return home to his wife, four year old daughter and 14 month old son.

I am so thankful we were able to provide him and his fellow Marines who were with him that day with Psalm 91 bandanas. He said it is still stained with blood, but it came home with him and will be a cherished possession of his for as long as he lives.

Being hit with shrapnel is a horrible, excruciatingly painful, damaging, deadly thing. Shrapnel is made up of jagged, small, sharp pieces of metal, sometimes glass, that will rip and tear into the body. It can embed itself in the body, and if one survives the blast, it may not be able to be removed surgically.

I learned something about that when I visited a wounded warrior event at Ft. Bragg. I was giving out bandanas and talking with the soldiers. I walked over to a soldier who had his elbows on his knees with his head resting in his hands. I asked him if he was all right. He told me when it gets cold, the shrapnel gets cold (it was winter time) and that it is very painful. He also said that the shrapnel was working its way out through his scalp that added to the pain. I never knew that shrapnel had a way of working itself to the surface, but it does. That is why surgery is not always used to remove pieces of shrapnel. Trying to get to it could, in itself, take the life of the soldier.

War is ugly and costly. The cost that is being paid by our men and women in uniform is very high. And because, in this day and time, we have such modern, miraculous ways to save lives, we have a whole generation of survivors of injuries in Iraq and Afghanistan who are suffering from the physical and emotional trauma of a war long in its duration. Oh how I pray that God's Word will be the balm that will bring healing to their souls and give them the strength and courage they need as they work through their experience.

CHAPTER 39

Take Care of My Family

I cannot complete this book without mentioning a very important person in the lives of our men serving in the military...their wives. Having been an army wife for 20 years, I understand the responsibilities that the military wife carries when she marries someone serving in our armed forces. Military wives play a very important, supportive, key part in the well-being of our troops and their performance of duty. Long gone are the days when it was said, "If the army wanted you to have a wife, they would have issued you one." It was finally acknowledged that if things are good on the home front, things will be good on the battle front, because if things are good at home, the one wearing the uniform is freed up to be a better soldier.

A MILITARY WIFE
Author Unknown

I wear no uniforms, no blues or army greens.
But I am in the military in the ranks that are rarely seen.
I have no rank upon my shoulders.
Salutes I do not give,
but the military world is the place where I live.
I am not in the chain of command; orders I do not get,
but my husband does, this I cannot forget.
I am not the one who fires the weapon,

who puts my life on the line,
but my job is pretty tough; I am the one that is left behind.
My husband is a patriot, a brave and pride filled man.
And the call to serve his country, not all understand.
Behind the lines I see the things needed to keep this country free.
My husband makes the sacrifice, but so do our kids and me.
I love the man I married. Soldiering is his life,
but I stand among the silent ranks known as the military wife.

I am a better person today because I was an army wife. All the families that we met along the way who came to mean so much to us became our family when we were so far from our own biological ones. We shared in one another's struggles and triumphs, our highs and our lows. There definitely is a certain kind of camaraderie that exists that can't really be explained... you just have to live it. And I still feel that connection when I am around military wives today. They are their own special, courageous breed and they have earned and need our support, encouragement and prayers. I have seen my daughter-in-law in action carrying out the duties of both mother and father while my son has been deployed. Being a single mom is not something she or any military wife relishes. But they manage somehow, accepting their responsibility without much complaint. They have a duty to perform also.

When soldiers are asked how we can help them, quite often you will hear them say, "Take care of my family." As we support our troops through Operation Bandanas and in other ways, don't forget this major support that they are asking of us...take care of their families!

CHAPTER 40

Somewhere Tonight
by Marilyn Swenson

Somewhere tonight
An American daughter, an American son
Treads unfamiliar soil
And dreams of home.

Somewhere a young girl is
Tenderly stowing away—into the suitcase of her mind,
Thoughts of beaus, fashionable dresses, late-night parties,
While she goes about her assigned duties,
Deliberately dismissing the lump in her throat
That makes it hard to swallow,
The fierce, rhythmic pounding of her heart,
Constant reminders that
Neither she nor her comrades
Are ever truly out of harm's way,
Demonstrating to herself,
And to all who care to see,
That courage is not determined by gender.

Somewhere a young boy is
Confronting his greatest fear,
His confident, imposing stance

(Inspired by months of rigorous training)
The surge of electrified energy
(Sparked by the demands of the moment)
Belying the faint, almost imperceptible,
Thread of a concern
That is doggedly wending its way to the
Forefront of his awareness:
"Will I conduct myself with honor?"
Instinctively, he reaches deep inside himself,
Summons the capacity to
Take captive every hint of discordant thought,
Every suggestion of confused clutter,
Liberating himself to
—Do what needs to be done
—Feel what needs to be felt
—See what needs to be seen.
And in the process,
—Unheralded by pomp or ceremony—
He becomes a man.

Somewhere tonight
An American mother, an American father
Wakes abruptly from a troubled sleep
And remembers.
Cherished images spew from hidden places:
A toddler weaving unsteadily across the floor
To the safety of outstretched arms;
A child, smiling through scraped knees and bruises,
Clutching a bicycle that has
—Uncharacteristically—
Remained upright during a trek across the front yard;
An adolescent struggling
To adjust to competing emotions,
Experimenting,
Looking for a comfortable way of being;

A teen driving away—alone—for the first time,
Being accepted into the flow
Of boisterous traffic;
A graduate, smiling,
Holding a diploma high in the air;
And always—standing off to the side,
A watchful parent
Poised, waiting to be needed.;
Then the latest entry:
An erect, uniformed figure
Waving good-bye,
Walking away into the unknown.
The pictures end;
Prayers fly upward to the One who sees the sparrow fall.
Rest comes with the assurance that
He is watching over all His children, wherever they are.

Somewhere tonight
An American hero,
—A veteran—is
Reading a newspaper,
Listening to a radio,
Watching a television,
Contemplating the war effort,
Wanting to contribute:
—To lend experience, support,
—To encourage, promote understanding,

Bristling at criticism from those who
Never marched to military cadence,
Never confronted hostile fire,
Grieving over the loss of respect
Towards the flag, the country
For which many have fought,
And not a few have died.

Somewhere tonight
I will—again—bow my head,
Thank my God for
—Every person who volunteers,
—Every person who waits behind,
—Every person who once served.
Because of their sacrifice,
I tread familiar soil unhindered, unafraid.

From *Taking the Long Way Home*, a collection of Christian poetry and prose written in 2006 by Marilyn Swinson, with contributions from Mollie Williams. Marilyn is a patriotic American who resides in Stoneville, NC. She recently published a book, *Scars of War*, based on interviews with more than forty veterans sharing their own, often horrifying accounts, of our nation's major battles from World War II through Iraq. Marilyn can be reached at mswinson@gmail.com.

Until They All Come Home

For more information about our ministry contact us at:

Operation Bandanas
PO Box 87356
Fayetteville, NC 28304
bandanas91@yahoo.com
www.operationbandanas.org

CPSIA information can be obtained at www.ICGtesting.com
Printed in the USA
BVOW071225240412

288503BV00002B/2/P